FOOTBALL CLUB
CHELSEA FOOTBALL CLUB
chelseafc.com
adidas
adidas
SAMSUNG

JOHN TERRY

When I was asked to write a foreword for this book, it was hard to know where to start. I've been coming to Stamford Bridge for well over a decade now, game in, game out.

It started during my days as a youth-team player, when I was a ball boy and then, when I signed my YTS contract, I was there cleaning the showers and hoovering the dressing room after games. After that I began coming here to play as a first-teamer. Now I get to live the ultimate experience – leading Chelsea out as captain.

It's still special every time I lead the team out of the tunnel with the armband on, hearing *The Liquidator* before each game and then looking up to see the supporters going through their chants for each player warming up before kick-off.

A lot has changed in football and stadiums down the years. But I'm sure if you asked the great captains of the past, from Roy Bentley to Ron Harris, Ray Wilkins, Dennis Wise, Marcel Desailly and all the others who have made Chelsea what it is, they will say those emotions were the same. That's the beauty of playing football for a club like this.

This place has become a huge part of my life and it always will be – so many memories are special to me. To name a few, I'll never forget signing my YTS contract on the pitch, making my first-team debut in the League Cup against Aston Villa, leading the team out as captain for the first time against Charlton, scoring the winning goal against Barcelona and, of course, lifting the Premier League trophy. It's just humbling to think that I'm a part of that and it makes me really proud.

SAMSUNG
SAMSUNG
DROGBA
11
LAMPARD
8
3
26
43

RON HARRIS

As the player who has ran out for Chelsea at Stamford Bridge more times than anybody else, it's fair to say it's a place that means an awful lot to me. I've always thought it's a brilliant stadium and it's played a huge role in my life, so I am proud to introduce this fantastic book to you.

My first memories of Stamford Bridge are back when I was just 11 years old. My older brother Allan signed for the club as an apprentice and, because I used to come and watch him play, they asked if I would like to be a ball boy. It was a big thrill just to be given a Chelsea tracksuit and run around on the greyhound track collecting the ball in front of up to 60,000 people.

Fast forward over 50 years from when I first came here and I still never miss a game, as I work for the club on matchdays in the hospitality suites. So this stadium has always been a big part of my life.

There have certainly been a lot of changes since the first time I came to the Bridge in the mid-Fifties. That is a sign of the times and shows the huge progress that has been made but, if I had seen how it would look now back in my playing days, I wouldn't have believed it. It has changed enormously since then.

Despite all the alterations, I can still see the old ground in today's Stamford Bridge. I can always visualise the old North Stand where I watched my brother, which used to shudder when the trains went past.

Chelsea has always been known for the Shed End and the hardcore supporters there and it's still the same in that way, even if it's not the same terracing any more. There has always been a fantastic atmosphere at the Bridge and that's down to you, the fans, who have been coming here over the years.

It's always been a ground that's great for mingling with supporters. In my playing days, us players would park our cars around the back and walk through the crowds of spectators to get to the changing rooms, with people asking for autographs and wishing us all the best for the game.

And nowadays I get there early and there's so many people who talk to you at the bar, the restaurant or the hotel. It's great that me and other ex-players can mix with the fans.

In fact, I think the atmosphere is better now the stands are a little bit more closed in. Don't forget, when I played there was a dog track around the pitch. The fans being so close makes for a tremendous atmosphere and it's especially great on European nights. Even in my playing days they were something special, with all the razzmatazz of playing against foreign opposition.

I'm immensely proud to have played more games here than anybody in history. I, like everybody who has been lucky enough to grace the turf at the Bridge, have so many amazing memories, which will never be taken away.

As fans, you will have your own special recollections and this book will hopefully bring some of those back for you.

CHELSEA FOOTBALL CLUB
adidas.com

CHELSEA
FOOTBALL CLUB

CONTENTS

BRIDGING THE YEARS

Much like the football club that appears there every other weekend, Stamford Bridge has a history that is as varied and unique as any stadium in the country. Obviously, there have been wholesale changes since Chelsea played their first-ever game there, almost three decades after its opening as an athletics venue in 1877, to its current incarnation.

However, there is one thing that will never change – the memories of each and every Chelsea fan, player and member of staff who has had the privilege of witnessing so many magical moments here.

Of course, all of the places you would expect to read about are covered in detail. How could we possibly produce a book about the home of Chelsea Football Club without finding out why the Shed End was the place to be in the Sixties and Seventies?

But, equally, the likes of Bobby Tambling, Joey Jones and Terry Venables delve even deeper than that to uncover the true character of the stadium in those rarely spoken about places of the ground. You'd never have guessed that the referee's room could become a home-from-home for a professional footballer...

Then there's the emotions that the Bridge stirs up in players and supporters alike. What does it feel like to walk down the tunnel and on to that hallowed turf in front of more than 40,000 people, all of whom have one common goal for the next 90 minutes? And then, when all is said and done, to lift the ultimate prize in English football – the Premier League trophy – in front of your own fans?

So join us as we take you on a journey around Stamford Bridge as seen through the eyes of the people who have helped make it such a special place to millions of people. We hope you enjoy reading the memories as much as we have compiling them.

ea Club

BRIDGE AHEAD

The external face of Stamford Bridge may have changed drastically over the decades, but the sight of the stadium has always been enough to stir the emotions of every fan. While most memories are forged on the other side of the turnstiles, for many the action begins on the approach down Fulham Road where excitement and expectation builds with every step...

CHELSEAFC
OFFICIAL MERCHANDISE
DOUBLE DEAL

FORECOURT KICK-ABOUTS

I remember the day before my debut we played five-a-side on the concrete at the front of Stamford Bridge. It was just a bit of a kick-about on the forecourt before we left to go to the station and get the train to Sunderland, we always did it before away games.

The legendary Peter Osgood said to me "just be careful Birch". I didn't know what he meant, but Dave Sexton gave out the bibs and I remember Peter Bonetti getting the ball and throwing it out to me. I was think this first touch as a Chelsea player has got to be good, even though it's just a bit of fun.

The next I knew I was coming around. Apparently I'd gone 15 feet up in the air and came round to a certain gentleman looking over me saying "welcome to Chelsea." Good old Chopper Harris.

He'd come straight in and kicked me up in the air so I got a rude awakening. I said to Osgood afterwards: "I know what you mean now." He just grinned and replied: "It's just his welcome to you. You did well because you didn't retaliate." But I don't know what I could have done because I was knocked out!

I couldn't believe it but that was my initiation at Chelsea. I didn't know it at the time, but those kick-abouts on the forecourt were a big part of things and nobody ever wanted to stop. Sexton would always be trying to get us on the train but we'd insist on one more goal.

- ALAN BIRCHENALL
EX-PLAYER 1967-1970

Upper Tier Gates 3-4
Upper Tier Gates 1-2
West Stand
Spackman Entrance

Welcome to ChelseaFC
OFFICIAL CHELSEA MERCHANDISE
adidas
100% CHELSEA

Lining up: Supporters queue for tickets outside the ground and (below) greeting their heroes and getting some autographs at an open training session

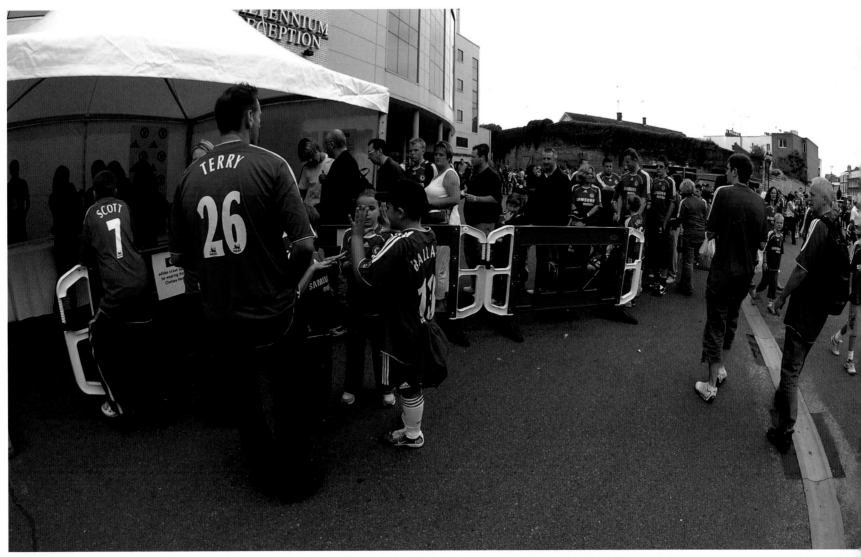

Popular event: Crowds gather for Fan Day at the Bridge while (below) matchgoers browse some club merchandise before passing through the turnstiles

East Stand: Fans gather for an evening kick-off

Ground force: Supporters head towards the West Stand entrance for Fan Day in August 2008 and (below) on a matchday three years earlier

Famous gateway: Fans pass through the Shed End turnstiles during the early 1980s

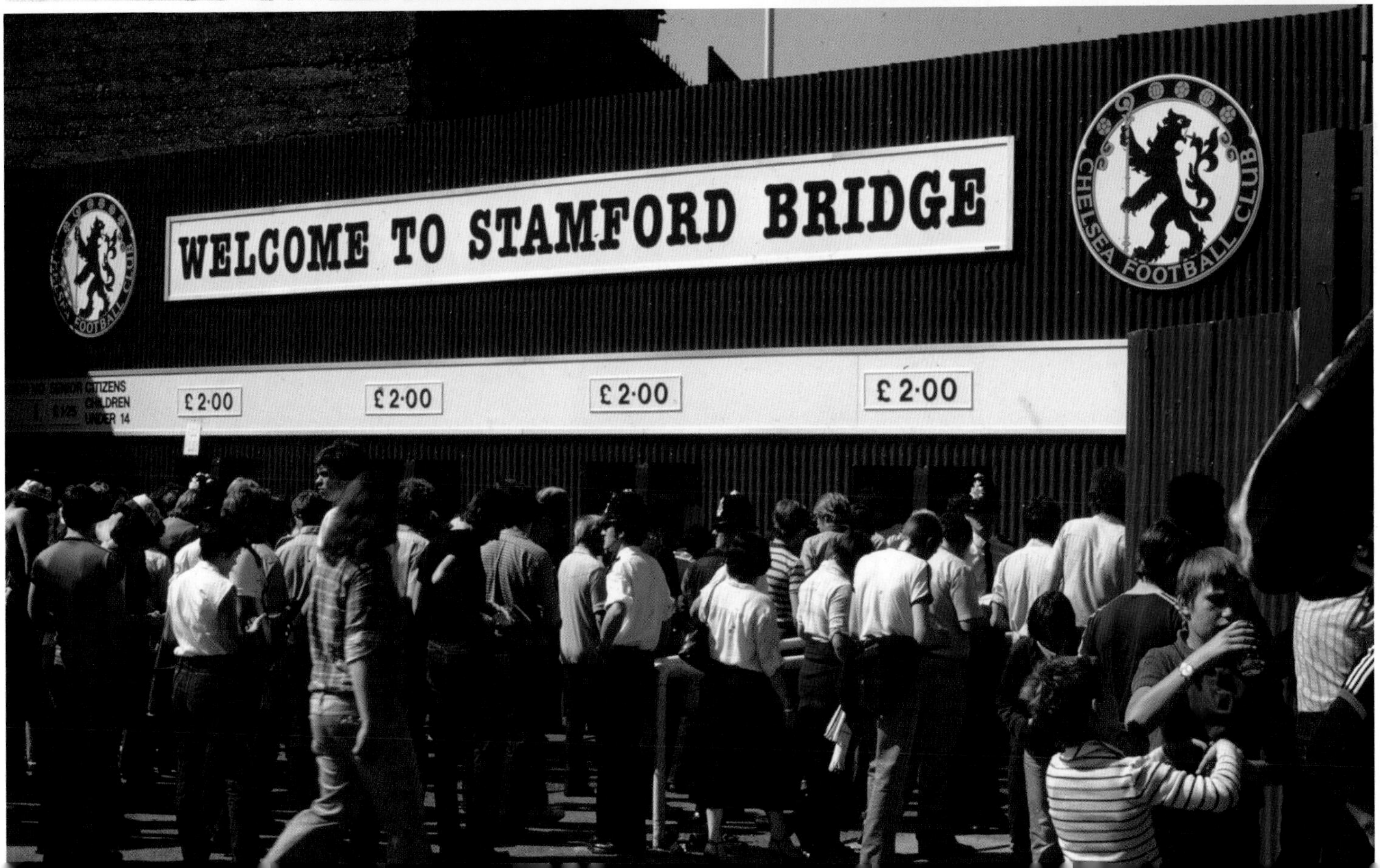

Right on queue: Chelsea fans wait outside Stamford Bridge for tickets ahead of the FA Cup replay with Leeds United in April 1970 and (below) a similar scene almost 40 years on as crowds head to the ground

WALKING WITH THE FANS

I lived at Chelsea Harbour, so I walked to the stadium for games. I'd get recognised by the supporters but it was fine because you can walk with them.

They're very respectful, they'd just say: "Hey Chapi, what's up? Good luck for today!" So they don't really bother you.

It was funny because I could never imagine walking to the Nou Camp in Barcelona with the fans. It wouldn't be dangerous, but there'd be too many people and it wouldn't be the best situation!

- ALBERT FERRER
EX-PLAYER 1998-2003

SMELL OF BURGERS

The old ground, back in the Seventies, might not have been everybody's cup of tea, but it had a different sort of character to today.

I remember I used to walk down the Fulham Road and that smell of burgers would hit you straight away. You knew the burgers were rank but it was a really comforting smell!

There was about a 200-yard walk as you approached the ground, it was always exciting and, not being funny, it was a bit scary at times back then.

- TREVOR NELSON
DJ/PRESENTER

Heading to the game:
Matchgoers pass through
Perry's Passage outside
Stamford Bridge

CFC
AC CONTROLS LTD
0800 521244

Window of opportunity: Ticketless Chelsea fans find a way to watch the game on TV through the windows of The Shed Bar during the Premiership match between Chelsea and Arsenal on September 8, 2001, while one supporter browses the headlines (below) as he awaits an evening kick-off

Imposing: The exterior of the East Stand

STAMFORD BRIDGE GROUNDS
CHELSEA
FOOTBALL & ATHLETIC CO. LTD.
GREYHOUND RACING
STAMFORD BRIDGE STADIUM
GREYHOUND RACING
THURSDAYS AND SATURDAYS AT 2·30 P.M.

Matchday commute: Chelsea's all-time leading goalscorer Bobby Tambling heads to the game on public transport, while (left) the old Stamford Bridge main entrance with its giant gates

GATEWAY TO AN AWESOME SIGHT

I think my favourite part of Stamford Bridge was the main entrance, when they had those massive gates there. In fact, the gates probably shielded the Bridge from the road. Now, when you get to the main entrance on Fulham Road, you see this massive stadium. Every time I'm over, even now, I get to that opening where you can see the hotel and the East Stand, it's such an awesome sight. It gets the juices going!

I can always remember the excitement when I first walked through there as a 15-year-old. The entrance in those days wasn't fantastic, it's more about where you were – the home of Chelsea Football Club. I've never lost that excitement and tingle you get when you go round the corner... it still does it to me now.

I saw a photo of me the other day from the Sixties when I was on the tube – that was the most embarrassing day! In those days the players weren't easily recognisable, it's not like today where everybody knows them.

I think I'd only been in the first team a year or so when the picture was taken and I used to get the tube from Wimbledon to Fulham Broadway. For matches, I'd travel in a bit early to avoid most of the crowd, so not too many recognised you. Those that did recognise you weren't sure you were who they thought you were. It's just how things were back in those days. We were just normal guys. In fact, when that picture was taken I might not have even had a car!

– BOBBY TAMBLING
EX-PLAYER 1959-1970

Stepping back:
The old Bovril Gate
entrance to the Shed End

Old and new: The former ivy-covered entrance to the offices and (below left) a model of the future stadium

IVY-CLAD OFFICES

Going to the offices at Stamford Bridge, which is where the hotel is now, they were quite quaint cottage-looking buildings with ivy on them. They were almost Victorian cottages and I remember ivy growing on the outside. It's always seemed huge from the outside and it always seemed too big for its space.

I remember Ken Bates, the first time I met him, showing me this model of what Stamford Bridge was going to be and this was part of his masterplan and, by me signing, I was becoming part of it – not that I was going to be putting down bricks or anything!

If I'm honest, I didn't think it would ever materialise, but it did and it's gone beyond that. You look at the facilities now and it's a very professional club and the players are very fortunate to have all of that support and infrastructure behind them.

– GRAEME LE SAUX
EX-PLAYER 1989-1993
& 1997-2003

Famous figure: Lynn Osgood with John Terry and Frank Lampard at the unveiling of her late husband's statue

STATUE OF HUGE STATURE

I was a nervous wreck before I saw the statue of Peter because you have in your mind's eye what it is going to look like, but having seen it, it's a thousand times better than I imagined.

It's all down to the fans and the club that we've got this statue. It was their vision and they pressed to have something like this outside of Stamford Bridge and it's absolutely fitting. It's amazing!

He'd love it, absolutely love it and I think we've done him proud. When I saw it, it was overwhelming, that is all I can say. It's just fantastic. It depicts him perfectly. It's definitely got his character and personality – The King of Stamford Bridge.

We're fantastically proud, he was a very special man and he deserves this very much so.

- LYNN OSGOOD

Warm welcome: Photographers gather outside Stamford Bridge on the day Roman Abramovich took over the club and (right) the Chelsea Village Hotel

BLUE SKIES

City panorama: A view of London from the rooftop of Stamford Bridge in May 1981

Aerial view: Stamford Bridge as seen from the Empress Tower Building at Earls Court in 1980, while (below left) the stadium in 1984 and (below right) in 2007

CHELSEA FOOTBALL CLUB
chelseafc.com
adidas
SAMSUNG
SAMSUNG

EAST STAND

A vintage vantage point for many matchgoers, the East Stand was the first to be constructed in the early 1900s, but its ambitious redevelopment in 1973 brought about spiralling costs and the club's temporary decline. It was, however, the envy of football stadia with a three-tier construction ahead of its time, while further modernisation has maintained its magnificence...

the global Ba lays Football face ook fan page
Join the global Barclays Footb
SAMSUNG
adidas

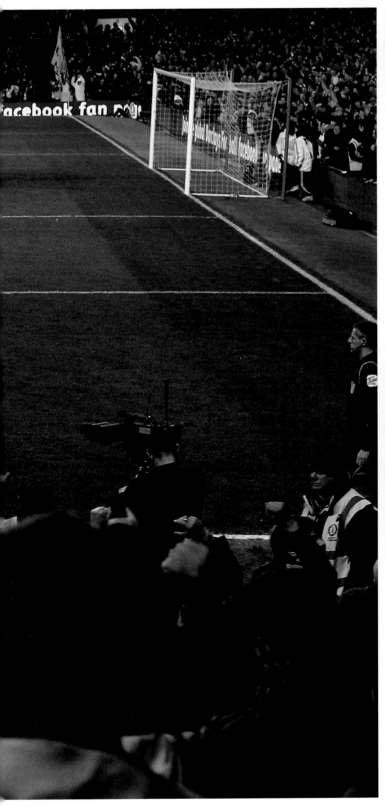

Up close and personal: A fan's view from the East Stand as David Luiz celebrates scoring against Manchester United; Mickey Thomas (above) recollects his own celebration in front of Gate 13 (top)

NOTORIOUS GATE 13

My home debut was against Sheffield Wednesday and it was the type of stuff you dream about. They were clear favourites to go up as champions, but we beat them 3-2 with me scoring twice and setting up the other. For my first, I put the ball through the keeper's legs and as I celebrated, Joey Jones just kept shouting "Gate 13, Gate 13" at me. It must have taken me 10 minutes to get out of the crowd – I went in with a gold chain and came back without it! I never thought about going in there again.

- MICKEY THOMAS
EX-PLAYER 1984-1985

Celebration time: Fans gather around the East Stand after promotion to the First Division

FAVOURITE CORNER

My favourite part of the ground was the East Stand, in the corner. You had a guy here, who was clerk of the works, called Harry Winston. And when I came here, I was playing for the schoolboys and Allan Harris, Terry Moore and Bert Murray all signed on, but I didn't sign for a while.

There was a lot of umming and ahhing about whether I'd sign, but when I came, Harry said: "I've got a right rubbish job for you now. I want you to go and sweep that stand!"

The others were in hysterics because it was the Monday after a game and it was an absolute tip! The other guys loved it. I'll always remember that because it was my initiation at Stamford Bridge... it's a bit different these days.

- TERRY VENABLES
EX-PLAYER 1960-1966

Star jumps: Terry Venables during a training session at the Bridge and (above) surveying the empty stadium in April 1965

Keeping watch: The old East Stand seats where Pat Nevin's dad would watch him in action (right); the seating area as it looks now (top); and Nevin goes on one of his famous runs against Newcastle in November 1983 (bottom)

SECRET SALUTE TO DAD

My dad missed one match in my Chelsea career – not bad considering he was a working man living in Glasgow and we tended to play in London's West End. On Saturdays he had to leave a couple of minutes before the end of each match to make sure he could get to Euston on time for the last train home, so we didn't usually get the chance to meet up afterwards.

We had an agreement, however, that in each game I would wave up to where I knew he was sitting in the main stand, pretty high and not far from the centre line – I got to know that spot very well.

There was, however, another secret signal for saying "Hello." In every game I allowed myself at least one totally self-indulgent dribble, which was a nod to the work my dad and I did day after day, year after year, on my dribbling skills as I grew up. After those mazy runs I would sneak a glimpse up to my dad and if I had thrown in a few decent dummies and went by a few defenders, there was a smile and a wink shared. Some fans of a certain age may remember a specific dribble the length of the field against Newcastle. Well, even that was one of those indulgences.

On the day I (unwillingly) left the club, I went up to that seat in the early evening all alone and sat there contemplating what I was leaving behind. The sun was setting over the old West Stand on that warm summer's day when the importance of that seat, and the incredible memories of those five years, came flooding back. I knew then that I might get more success during the rest of my career but would never find more happiness or feel more at home.

- PAT NEVIN
EX-PLAYER 1983-1988

Customary position: A lone Chelsea pensioner sits in the main stand

Bog standard: Early East Stand facilities included the toilets (above) and a matchday creche (below)

CHELSEA FOOTBALL CLUB
chelseafc.com
adidas
adidas
SAMSUNG
SAMSUNG
adidas
adidas
SAMSUNG
SAMSUNG
adidas

Baby Blue: A young Jason Cundy, and later in his media role

MIXING WORK AND PLEASURE

My favourite part of Stamford Bridge has to be the East Stand, which is where I watched my first game from at the age of six and I still sit in pretty much the same place now when I'm working with the media at games. It has the same feeling and I get the same buzz I did all those years ago.

My dad took me to my first match against Charlton in November 1976 for my sixth birthday. I remember the whole build-up – travelling up there on the tube, walking from the station to the ground and seeing it for the first time. There's a unique smell going to the match as well and I can still feel the energy that was around the ground when I think about it now.

Then there was the moment when we walked up the steps, which were never ending for a six-year-old, and looked down on the green grass lit up by the floodlights – it was just remarkable. I can still see it now and have such vivid memories. I was in complete awe of what was around me. The whole day, with Chelsea winning as well, was just brilliant and, from that day onwards, I was absolutely hooked.

– JASON CUNDY
EX-PLAYER 1988-1992

Personnel touch: Chelsea staff and players line up in front of the East Stand in 1975

First look: Micky Droy and David Hay share a joke in front of the newly-completed East Stand ahead of the 1974/75 season

WEST STAND

The 13,500-seat West Stand, incorporating the Millennium Suites, opened in 2001 and marked the completion of Stamford Bridge's redevelopment which began back in 1973...

chelseafc.com
L CLUB
chelseafc.com

Changing face of fashion: The dapper attire of the average matchgoer gave way to a more casual look during the '80s and '90s

FASHION PARADE

I started going to football with my mates in the Eighties and back then you had to make the effort or you just didn't fit in, which used to amuse my dad no end when he saw me spending ages blow-drying my hair and sorting what jewellery to wear to go to a football match!

It was about that time Chelsea fans decided to start sitting down at games and we'd get tickets for the benches at the front of the West Stand if we couldn't afford seats in the East Lower.

We often sat there talking about the latest casual clothes rather than the football, like something out of the gossip pages of girls' magazines.

Back then it was more like a fashion show than a sporting occasion and the Bridge was the home of the 'Casual' - there were terraces and stands full of young men prancing around like peacocks.

It was the time when the tracksuit, the polo neck, the golf jumper and wedge haircuts hit football grounds big time, post-skinheads and donkey jackets.

I can still remember the absolute joy when I bought my first Tacchini tracksuit top – it cost me £45 from Stuarts in Shepherd's Bush. I bought it on Saturday morning and had it on at the football by the same afternoon.

- TIM LOVEJOY
TV PRESENTER

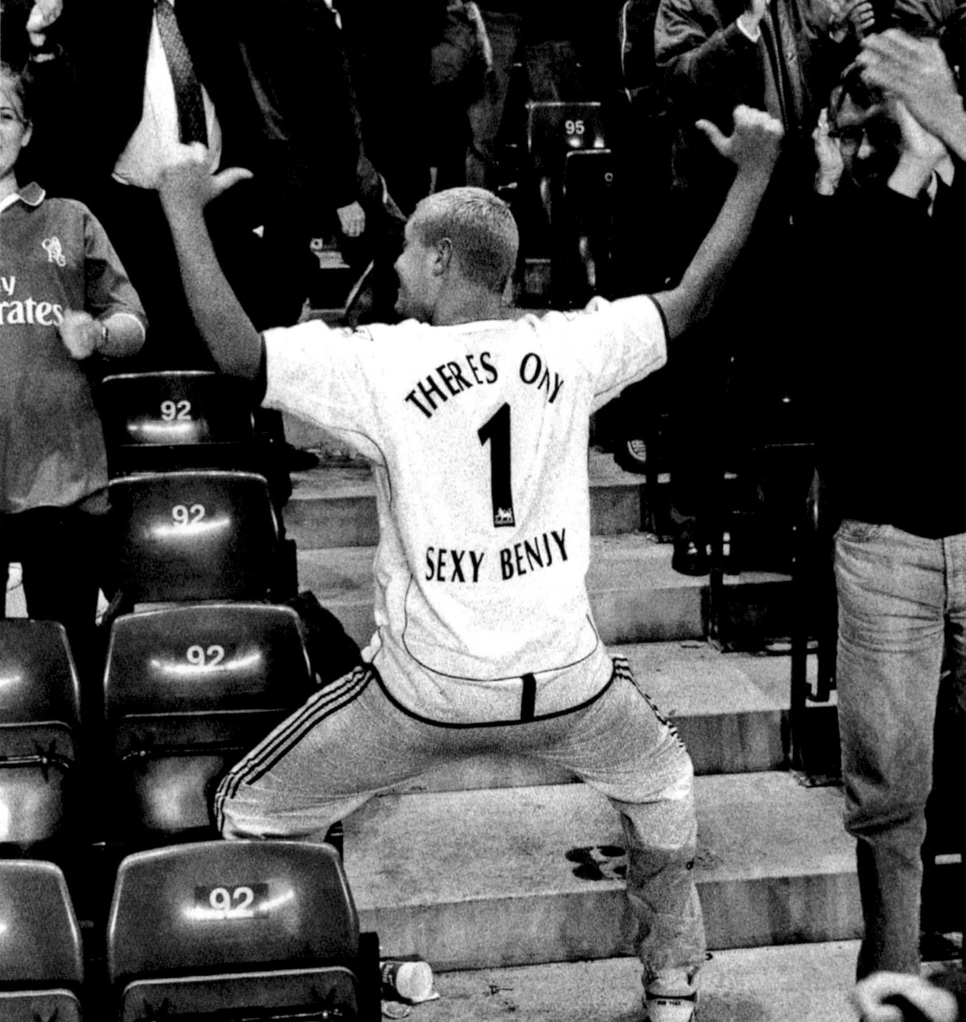

Face in the crowd:
Chelsea fan Stuart Deabill (circled) mixes with the 'Casuals' in the West Stand in 1984

CASUAL MOVEMENT

The funny thing about this picture is that I didn't know it existed until the late Nineties. I was amazed and instantly transported to the game, season and look of April 1984 – and was just pleased that I had a decent shirt on, even if I was catching flies! It was Pierre Cardin, which was in for a week, such was the heady times of being a teenage Chelsea Casual.

Out of all the games to be photographed at, it was the day we got promoted against one of our bitterest rivals, Leeds.

I always get asked who the fella in the Lacoste jacket is. Apart from Martin, from my old manor Northolt who is halfway back, I don't know anyone else in the photo.

Not only was it such a momentous day beating Leeds 5-0, but that whole season is still my favourite in over 30-odd years of going to Chelsea. I only missed two games all season and I forged friendships over those nine months that still last to this day.

Also, walking into the West Stand back then was such a fashion parade that you had to be up to scratch on the clobber front otherwise you'd be slaughtered by your mates for letting the side down with a tired pair of Kickers or last year's Diamond Pringle... And definitely no replica shirts!

I've still got a season ticket and the last few years have been stuff of dreams, but being 17, cocky, casual and carefree, cheering on that beautiful team, will never be beaten for me. The photo will always remind me of that.

- STUART DEABILL,
TEENAGE CHELSEA 'CASUAL'

Old layout: The wooden seats which once occupied the West Stand (right); and fans navigate their way down the steps in 1990 (below)

Loud speaker: Ken Bates appeals to fans in the West Stand not to invade the pitch in the second half of the game which secured Chelsea's promotion to the First Division in 1984

YOUNG BARRIER BRIGADE

From the age of six, my dad would take me to Fulham one week and Chelsea the next. My main recollections are of the West Stand, which was all terracing back then. In those days, when you'd have huge crowds at the Bridge, you tried to get a little kid like me onto one of the barriers on the terracing.

People actually used to pass the kids from the back over everybody's heads down to the edge of the greyhound track, but I think my dad was always worried about being able to get me afterwards!

The atmosphere at Stamford Bridge back in the Fifties was amazing and I just remember the noise. In those days, you'd quite often be stood next to people with a rattle, so there was such a racket going around the place.

When I first went, I used to think it was noisy, but after a while you get used to it and you start to enjoy every minute of it.

– JOHN DEMPSEY
EX-PLAYER 1969-1978

Blues legend: Peter Bonetti acknowledges his warm reception at Stamford Bridge; the executive boxes housed in the West Stand (top)

FAMILY OCCASION

I come back to Stamford Bridge a lot and still work for the club here after 30 years. I even went on a stadium tour with my four brothers.

It was on the day which would have been my father's 100th birthday if he was still with us and we wanted to go and see all the places where we grew up, the places that were important to him and reminded us of him.

One of those places was the Bridge, where he obviously used to come a lot to see me play back when I was younger. He used to sit in the West Stand when I was playing and my brothers would go with him quite a lot.

There are a lot of good family memories for all of us at the Bridge and it still feels like a second home for me, even though it's changed a lot in stature.

- PETER BONETTI
EX-PLAYER 1960-1975 & 1976-1979

Net outlook: A view of the West Stand from behind the Matthew Harding Stand goal

Building for the future: Cranes tower over Stamford Bridge as the finishing touches are made to the new-look West Stand

Room for improvement: A more conservative looking West Stand prior to its reconstruction in 1993

adidas
SAMSUNG
CHELSEA
SUPER FR
MPARD 8
JT CAPTAIN,LEADER,LEGEND
PRIDE
SAMSUNG
adidas

MATTHEW HARDING/ NORTH STAND

Previously the North Stand, the Matthew Harding Stand takes its name from the former Chelsea director who helped transform the club in the early 1990s before his death in 1996. It has undergone a series of transformations but the one constant has been its vocal support from the banner-bearing supporters...

High life: The North Stand is almost deserted after is was closed following reports of it 'shuddering' during a match in 1971

Winter scene: Snow covers the North Stand in 1968

CHRISTMAS CRACKER

My father brought me to Stamford Bridge for the first time, believe it or not, on Christmas Day, 1957. I saw Jimmy Greaves score four goals in a 7-4 win over Portsmouth and, as we left the ground, my father said you'll never see another 17-year-old play as well as that again. Little did I know that a few years later I would see arguably an even better 17-year-old wearing the Chelsea blue, and that, of course, was Peter Osgood.

I can also remember sitting in that old North Stand on the corner – the one raised on stilts – when Chelsea played Southampton once. Osgood scored one of the greatest goals I've seen in over 50 years of watching football. If I tell you he beat seven players on that wonderful run, you've got to believe me! Peter Bonetti won't want reminding of the final score, though – Chelsea 2, both scored by Osgood, Southampton 6! Never mind...

– JOHN MOTSON
FOOTBALL COMMENTATOR

Construction: The new North Stand begins to take shape as Nigel Spackman battles against Coventry in November 1994

On the up: Fans in the North Stand celebrate promotion to the First Division during a 4-0 victory over Hull City on May 14, 1977

Double act: Ken Bates and Matthew Harding in the new North Stand and (below) tributes are left in memory of the former Blues director in October 1996

LUCKY END

I love the Matthew Harding Stand, which was known as just the North Stand before Matthew sadly passed away in 1996. I remember playing in the first game after they opened it in November 1994 – it was against Everton, but we lost 1-0. And I scored the first-ever goal at that end, too, against Charlton in the FA Cup.

I always liked playing at that end, whether I scored goals there or not! It always seemed to be jam-packed, lots of noise and just a nice part of the stadium. A lot of people talk about the Shed End, but you've got to remember that was still under reconstruction, so you had the temporary seating there.

In fact, my favourite two goals for Chelsea were against Liverpool and they both came at the North Stand end, so I guess it was kind of a lucky part of the ground for me.

I knew Matthew Harding quite well, he was around the team a lot, especially when Glenn Hoddle was the manager because him and Glenn were good friends. He was a very jovial character, very down to earth – just a nice human being.

- JOHN SPENCER
EX-PLAYER 1992-1997

EMOTIONS RUNNING HIGH

The first game after Matthew Harding's death was against Spurs and it was just a roller-coaster of emotions. It was so emotional in the dressing room before the game and when we laid down the flowers before the game. Matthew was a friend to the lads. Myself and Johnny Spencer had actually arranged to go up to Scotland with him to watch Rangers in the Champions League shortly before he passed away.

Then there was the euphoria of scoring and then 10 minutes later you're lying there with a broken leg. Once that happened it was a nightmare, I had so many injuries after that.

It was the most emotional game I've ever played in, without a doubt.

- DAVID LEE
EX-PLAYER 1988-1998

CYPRUS BLUES
CHELSEA FC
ONE LIFE
ONE LOVE
ONE CLUB
CAREFREE SINCE 1905
CHELSEA FOOTBALL CLUB
MATTHEW HARDING'S
BLUE & WHITE ARMY
One Hundred Years
Chelsea FC
CHELSEA
SUPER
OF LONDON
adidas

CRAZY GANG

My favourite part of the stadium is the part where the fans sit. That is what I love about Chelsea, the fans are all around you and singing, it is special. Especially the Matthew Harding stand, that is where the fans are crazy. That is what gives the link between the players and the fans and you can always hear them and that is where we go when we want to smile and celebrate with the fans. For me, that is the best, because the fans are all crazy there and you can see them behind the goal and hear them singing always.

- MARCEL DESAILLY
EX-PLAYER 1998-2004

Boys in blue: Police guard the goalmouth as fans in the North Terrace celebrate promotion back to the First Division in 1977 by running onto the pitch

adidas
SAMSUNG
chelseafc.com
CHELSEA FC
USA T-SHIRT SALE - UP TO 50% OFF
USA T-SHIRT SALE
UP TO 50% OFF

SHED END

Home of the most vocal, diehard Blues during its terraced days, the Shed has a special significance and religious-like resonance at the Bridge. Originally the Fulham Road End, the south side stand still conducts an orchestra of sound on matchdays, even though it has been accommodating a section of away fans since 2005...

Motor home: Cars belonging to the disabled fans are visible on the open expanse behind the Shed goal in 1992 (above) and a distant view of the action from the Shed End terraces in the 1970s (right)

SPACE BEHIND THE GOAL

The Shed was quite far back from the pitch. In fact the disabled supporters used to park their cars there. I can remember doing the warm-up before the game and you'd have the fans driving up, it was amazing. That goes to show how large that area was.

Actually, on a Friday we'd train at Stamford Bridge sometimes and we would use the grass area behind the goal at the Shed End to play five-a-side. It was that big! We'd do sprints at the away end and then head down the other end for a bit of five-a-side.

– NIGEL SPACKMAN
EX-PLAYER 1983-1987 & 1992-1996

BOY BALL TO BRIDGE STAR

I went to the Bridge for the first time as a nine-year-old and stood in the Shed End. Little did I know that two years later I'd meet up with a certain Gwyn Williams, who invited me for trials at the club and I fell in love with Chelsea straight away.

I started ball-boying when I was 13. The job went to Gwyn's favourite players and for me it was such a massive buzz. I was standing in front of such a big crowd and I felt so privileged to be able to do it. I saw it as an important part of my development.

I used to like going behind the goals at the Shed End. There was a lot of space between the fans and the goal in those days, the track was still there – it seemed like the fans were miles away. But I just loved the atmosphere, so when the ball boys had to queue up, I made sure I got to the front and I'd just make a dash for the Shed. It always seemed like most of the goals were scored there, too.

The funny thing is, we'd be standing in front of a load of cars, because that's where the disabled fans used to park.

Fortunately, I never made any mistakes as a ball boy – well, not that I can remember.

- FRANK SINCLAIR
EX-PLAYER 1990-1998

Set back: The view from the Shed End terraces on a sunny August day in 1983

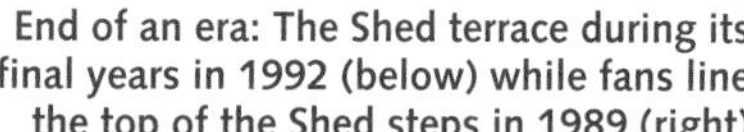

End of an era: The Shed terrace during its final years in 1992 (below) while fans line the top of the Shed steps in 1989 (right)

VOLUME OF SUPPORT

I first went to the Bridge in 1971 when we beat Blackpool 2-1 and I can't remember any of the football at all. I just remember being fascinated by the people – I was five years old and I'd never seen that many people.

That's really all I can remember about it, just the noise and thinking how loud it was in the Shed! It was only when I sat outside the Shed that I realised that no-one can actually hear you because it was so vast and distant. You needed about 40,000 to get Stamford Bridge kicking back then.

– JOHNNY VAUGHAN
TV/RADIO BROADCASTER

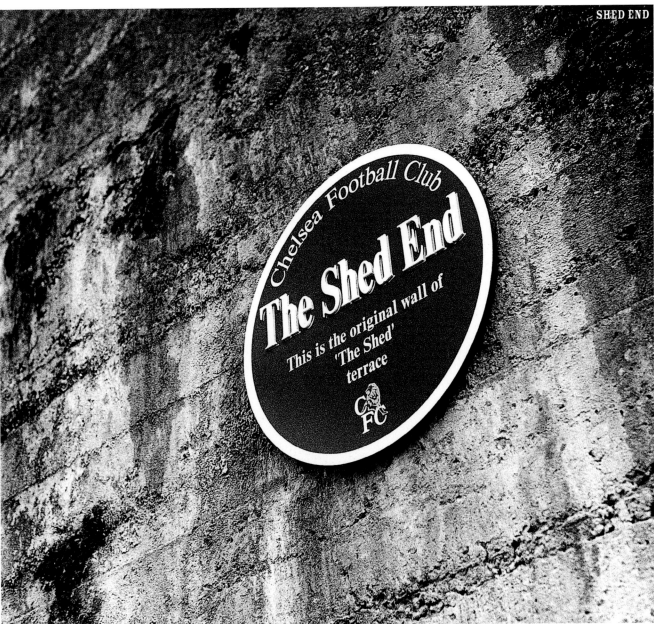

Chip off the old block:
The original Shed End wall is observed with this plaque and (left) the terrace in full swing back in 1980

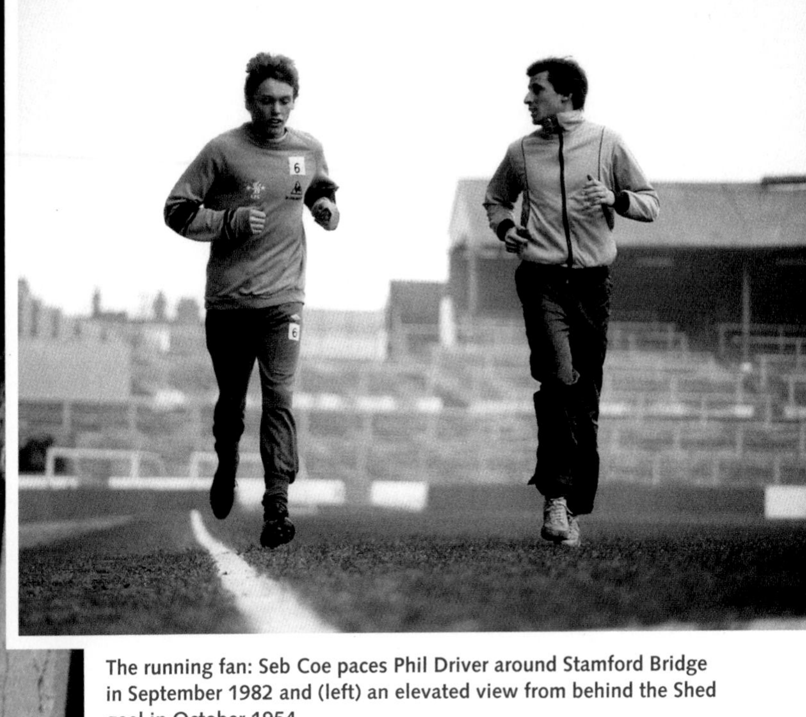

The running fan: Seb Coe paces Phil Driver around Stamford Bridge in September 1982 and (left) an elevated view from behind the Shed goal in October 1954

SHED SOME MEMORIES

For my first game I sat on what a few fans will still remember as the old benches in what is now the West Stand towards where the Matthew Harding Stand is.

But then, when I got a bit older, I started going on my own when I was staying in London with grandparents and that kind of thing, and I would go in the Shed End.

Then, when I got a little bit of prosperity, I got a season ticket and started sitting in the East Stand and I did that for a few years, but then my natural traction was to go back towards the Shed, which of course then was all-seater. I've been there ever since and I go there with my kids. All my kids are Chelsea fans, so we've got five season tickets now. That's what we do at weekends.

I get there as often as I can and, funnily enough, the people I now know at football as the permanent fixtures, are the people I started to meet in the Seventies. A lot of the people I sit with I originally stood in the Shed End with as a kid with and we've all grown up together watching Chelsea.

– LORD SEBASTIAN COE
POLITICIAN & FORMER ATHLETE

Crowd control: Police attempt to calm the supporters during the infamous 1984 Milk Cup semi-final clash with Sunderland and (below) a pitch invader interupts the game

IN TIMES OF TROUBLE

I think I was about 15 when I saw my first game at Stamford Bridge. It was in 1984 and it was the infamous Milk Cup semi-final second leg against Sunderland. I pestered my dad to get us tickets and it turned out to be an absolute riot! It really was a bad night for Chelsea both on and off the field and, looking back, I probably should have been put off because of the trouble.

Instead, a couple of years later I started to go regularly both home and away. It was quite hairy going to watch Chelsea in those days, but I loved being in the middle of the Shed, singing all the songs. At the same time, I can also remember some pretty bleak nights, like one midweek game against Oxford United when only 7,000 showed up and we drew 1-1.

Whenever my mates get frustrated at games now, I always remind them about that because we've got so much more to be cheerful about now.

– GRAHAM THORPE
FORMER CRICKETER

Cheer we go: The Shed in full celebration (left & top) after Chelsea's 5-0 victory over Leeds in April 1984 secured them promotion to the First Division in emphatic style; Ken Bates addresses the supporters during that momentous match (bottom)

BETTER THAN THE KOP

I loved the Shed. That's where my song came from: "His name is Tommy Baldwin and he's the leader of the team..." They always seemed to love me and I loved them – it really was mutual.

They gave us so much support and I always tell everyone that the fans in the Shed were better than the Kop! I loved going on the pitch, looking over and seeing them all lively and singing. And even when things weren't going well, the fans cheered us on.

I don't know if I scored more goals at that end than the other, I'm still trying to work out the average! But I definitely loved scoring there... I'd stick my hand up in the air and run to them.

I was proud to play for Chelsea and have the Shed behind me. And after I finished playing, I went and stood in the Shed myself.

During my playing days, we'd be sat up in the old North Stand – when it was windy it used to sway a bit! So that's where the players had our tickets, but I was always pining to be among the fans in the Shed.

– TOMMY BALDWIN
EX-PLAYER 1966-1974

Loyal servant: John Hollins gazes across Stamford Bridge as his playing career winds down in 1984

IN THE THICK OF IT

The Shed End is very special to me because of one of the games when I was manager. We were playing Aston Villa and we hadn't won in the last three home games. It was two days after Christmas and there was a lot "paper talk" saying the Shed weren't with us.

So I decided, although I didn't tell anyone, that before the game starts I would do my team talk, let the players walk out and then walk up to the Shed. Security would never have allowed me to do it, but I did it anyway.

I walked up and into the Shed and everyone was looking round and asking what I was doing there. I told them I'd heard they'd been giving me stick, but they all said they were behind me.

We went 2-0 up and just before half-time I got out, zoomed down and got in the dressing room before the players got back, and said to them: "That's more like it, and obviously you've got the supporters on your side as well now."

We ended up beating them 4-1 and went on a good run after that. Things did change that day, we had a little bit of luck and the crowd got behind us, but it's just one of those things.

Security said I was mad, but if we'd lost I would have had to face the fans in the end anyway, and it worked out well on the day.

For me, the Shed End was the place that everything came from, especially the noise and the opinions, so you might as well go straight in there and face it.

I sat back on the bench for the second half and gave them a wave in the Shed straight away. It's just one of those good memories.

- JOHN HOLLINS
EX-PLAYER 1961-1975 & 1983-1984
EX-MANAGER 1985-1988

Fan power: The changing face of the Shed End as fans flock to the terraces in 1980 (top); form a swarm of support in 1985 (right) and cheer on the Blues in 1994 (bottom)

Match momento: Didier Drogba gives his shirt to a fan in the Shed End after the Premier League game between Chelsea and Everton in December 2010

CLOSER TO THE ACTION

At the time I was playing, it was the Shed End that you remember best. That was one of the big memories I took away from Chelsea, they were never quiet and kept going.

The only thing I'd probably say is that it's much better now at the ground with the crowd being much closer to the pitch. You got a lot more atmosphere in the Shed when you were standing, but with the way the ground is now, with people close in, you get a really good atmosphere for the players when they're playing, it is a lot better on the pitch.

- IAN BRITTON
EX-PLAYER 1972-1982

Crowd pleasers: Colin Lee and Clive Walker celebrate in front of the Shed during the Division Two match against Derby County in August 1983

LIKE FATHER, LIKE SON

My dad supported Juventus when he was growing up, but he moved to England in his 20s and settled on Chelsea as his team. Like many things in life, especially when you're young, you follow what your father does.

So I think I would have probably been eight when I first started coming to the Bridge and, like so many others, it was in the Shed.

It was the era of guys like Clive Walker and Mickey Droy, and every time my dad brought me along, we seemed to win, so he used to try and get me to go as often as possible. But this was the early Eighties and Chelsea weren't winning every week by any stretch of the imagination, which tells you I wasn't going enough!

- LAWRENCE DALLAGLIO
FORMER RUGBY UNION PLAYER

CHELSEA
FOOTBALL
CHELSEAFC

FANFARE

Behind every great club, lies great fans. The famous twelfth man has played a prominent part in Chelsea's history, cheering the club onto their greatest glories both at home and across the continent...

Roar of the crowd: Frank Lampard wheels away in celebration

OVERWHELMED BY SUPPORT

The support from the stands is massive for me. Seeing my banner was huge and I'm sure John would say the same. Those sorts of things are kept aside for Osgoods and Zolas, quite rightly so, and it's great to have my own banner.

Let's be honest, there's no better feeling for me than running out for a game and hearing people singing my name, or if I score a goal and people are celebrating. If people think I should have a banner, it's an extra step from that. It's a huge deal and I've got a great bond with Chelsea fans, so obviously it's nice for me.

It gets my back up when I hear talk about Chelsea fans having no history, that they're all bankers who just turn up and watch or whatever – it normally comes from fans of other London clubs. It's a load of rubbish, you only understand Chelsea fans when you're at the club and I think there is something about them.

I've never heard them get right on someone's back, boo them and destroy them, never. Don't get me wrong, they can moan and groan a little bit, but that's normal, we all get upset watching games.

They are always there, they travel fantastically well and those comments are just the jealousy factor of fans of other teams. The main thing is that they don't get on anyone's back and some clubs, given what we've been given and being elevated to where we are now, would be moaning 'We should be winning' after 20 minutes at 0-0.

But Chelsea fans are a little bit different, probably because they've been through a lot before I was here, where they've sat down and watched a Division Two team in a stand that was 30 yards away from the pitch. So now they can't believe what's happening here, they go with it and, like me, they think it's fantastic.

- FRANK LAMPARD

SAMSUNG

TERRY
26

NO SMOKING
JOHN TERRY'S
BLUE ARMY
CHELSEA LOYAL
SAMSUNG

FLYING THE FLAG

The likes of myself and Frank have been here a long time and have a good relationship with the fans and know what this club means to them.

But to see our flags up and our own songs being sung... honestly, it makes the hairs on the back of my neck stand up and I get goosebumps. Even when they sing Frank's song... the excitement from it is unbelievable.

– JOHN TERRY

Warm reception: Ron Harris acknowledges the fans while Gianfranco Zola (left) shows his appreciation as he brings his Chelsea playing career to an end in May 2003

WAVE OF SUPPORT

For me, and I'm sure for a lot of the ex-players, our best memories are the supporters down at the Shed End in the terraces. It was a big thing years ago when there were no seats, just terraces, and when we used to go out on to the pitch, one of the first things we used to do is go over and wave to the spectators in the Shed.

The lads always used to go over and wave, and the supporters would sing the players' names, and that was part and parcel of the game, especially at the Bridge. There is still a stand at the Bridge called the Shed End, but to me the Shed will always mean the terracing from years ago that was taken over by the real die-hard Chelsea supporters from my era.

– RON HARRIS
EX-PLAYER 1961-1980

Supporters' salute: Peter Bonetti gives a wave to fans in the Shed before his last league game for the Blues in May 1979

Crowd pleasers: Players applaud the Chelsea fans ahead of the 5-0 victory over Leeds in April 1984 (right); Frank Lampard does likewise in 2010 (top); while Clive Walker celebrates with supporters after scoring against Oldham in May 1980 (bottom)

Champions: John Terry raises the Premier League trophy towards the fans in 2005

Going up: Fans swarm onto the pitch as the club celebrate promotion to the First Division in 1984

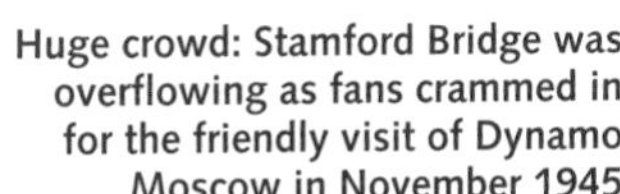

Huge crowd: Stamford Bridge was overflowing as fans crammed in for the friendly visit of Dynamo Moscow in November 1945

FRIENDLY FRENZY

When we played Dynamo Moscow in a friendly, the fans were sitting on the dog track – there must have been 70,000 there. It must have made for quite a picture.

–PETER BRABROOK
EX-PLAYER 1954-1962

adidas
SAMSUNG
chelseafc.com
SAMSUNG
adidas
SAMSUNG
SKY SPORTS
SAMSUNG
thomascook.com
adidas
SAMSUNG
chelseafc.com
SAMSUNG
adidas
adidas
adidas
adidas
adidas

Lengthy line-up: A group of fans join the Chelsea team as they attempt to create a world-record squad photograph in 2006 and (below) the supporters in full voice on matchday

Restricted view: Two Chelsea fans try to get a glimpse of the action in 1998 and (right) supporters storm onto the pitch after the Blues secure promotion in April 1984;
Below: Fans run to join Colin Lee's goal celebration in the 2-0 FA Cup fifth round victory over Liverpool in February 1982 and (right) more goal celebrations from high up in the stands

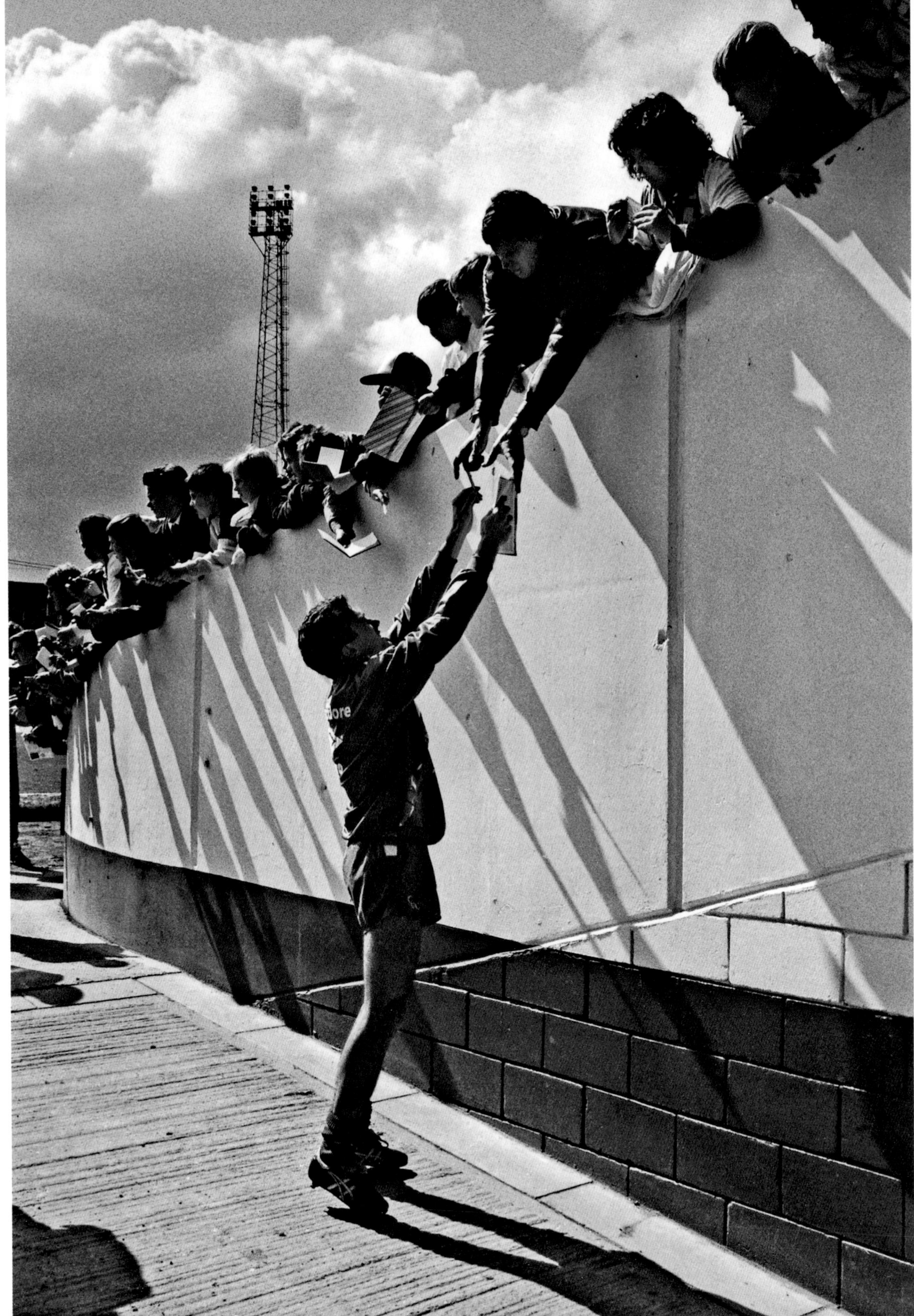

Fan favours: Tony Dorigo signs autographs as he heads back down the tunnel in 1991

CORRIDORS OF POWER

New home: Fernando Torres tours the Stamford Bridge offices as he agrees his transfer

TAKING NEXT STEP UP

I think when you make a decision this important you must be sure you can do it, otherwise it's not worth moving to a club like Chelsea. I was sure – I was waiting for an opportunity like this because I felt that I needed to make a step forward in my career and try to show that there is one more level.

– FERNANDO TORRES

Pen to paper: Andriy Shevchenko signs for Chelsea watched by former Chief Executive Peter Kenyon and Club Secretary David Barnard in 2006, while the duo also oversee the signing of Nicolas Anelka in January 2008 (below)

Signing in: Alex goes through the formalities of his Chelsea move with David Barnard in 2007 and (below) Chief Executive Ron Gourlay witnesses the signature of Fernando Torres on January 31, 2011

Contract extension:
Frank Lampard signs a new five-year deal in the Chelsea boardroom in August 2008

Welcome speech: Jose Mourinho with new signing Michael Ballack in 2006 (left); Fernando Torres takes a call in the Stamford Bridge meeting room (top); Ashley Cole is welcomed to the club by former Chief Executive Peter Kenyon in August 2006 (bottom)

ALL CHANGE

The hub of pre and post-match activity, the Stamford Bridge home dressing room is both the arena for big game build-up and final whistle reflection. It is also a place where gameplans are forged, spirits are lifted and, if you get it right, champagne is uncorked...

CECH
1
8

Players' entrance: The Chelsea squad arrive at Stamford Bridge and (below) relaxing in the dressing room

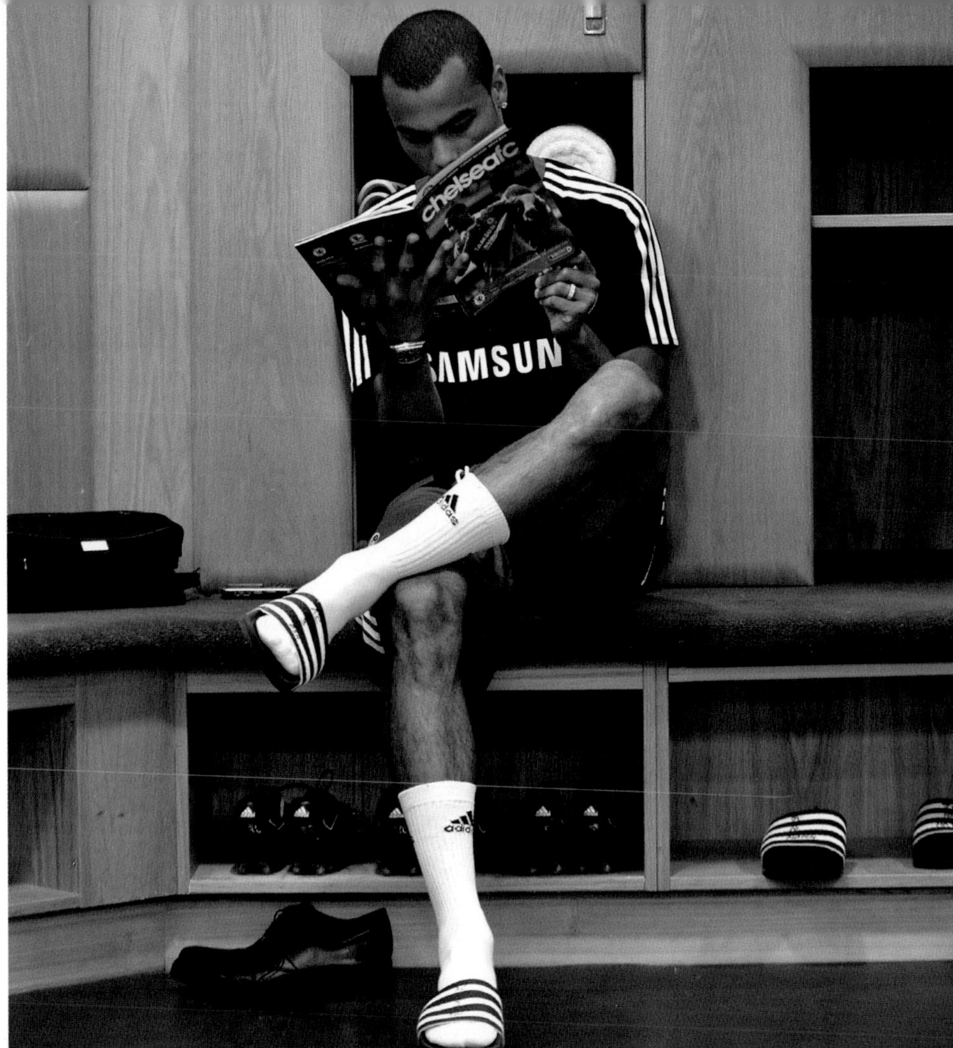

Reading material: Ashley Cole and Alex (below) look over the programme ahead of kick-off

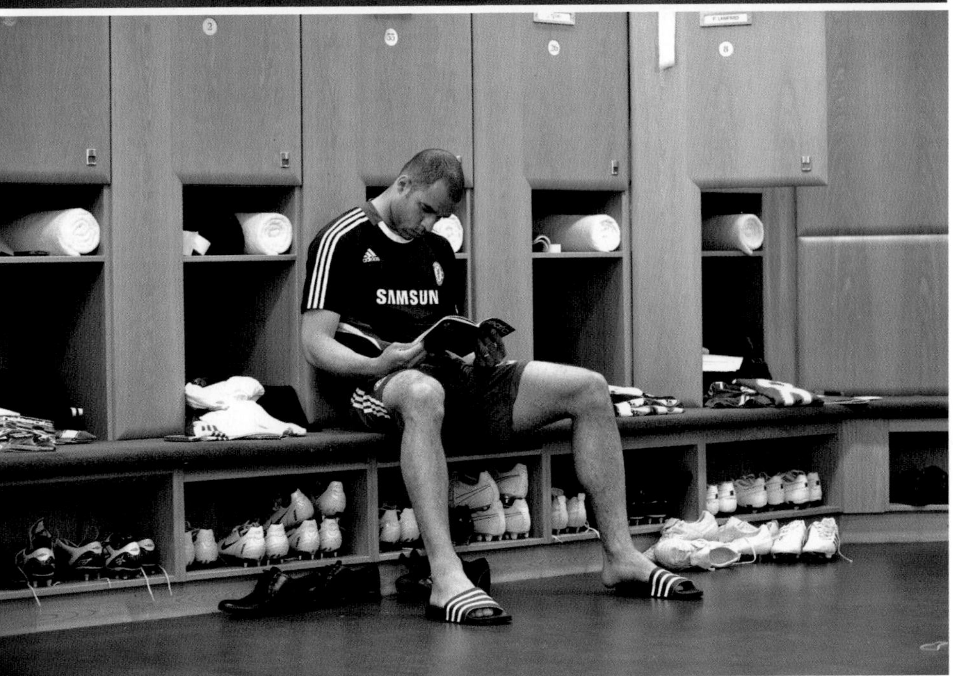

SECOND HOME

The atmosphere we have every game at home is special and, of course, the people.

When you stay at a club for such a long time, you will miss the people when the moment comes that you have to leave.

This is like a second home for me now – I have had so many good moments, good laughs and, of course, I have loved playing football here.

When you arrive in the stadium before the game, you see your team-mates in the dressing room, have a chat, listen to some music and relax. After that you focus yourself for the game.

– PAULO FERREIRA

Behind the scenes: The entrance to the Chelsea dressing room and (below) Didier Drogba, Mikel and Fernando Torres lace up their boots ahead of the match

Pre-match preparation: Kits are laid out ahead of the players' arrival (above & below left); Michael Essien in the dressing room as it gets a sweep (below)

Kickabout: Players perform keepy-ups ahead of kick-off

PRE-MATCH KEEPY-UPS

One of my strong memories of the pre-match build-up at Stamford Bridge is Peter Bonetti always going into the old gym and keeping the ball up before the game. For a goalkeeper, Peter Bonetti was one of the most skilful players here at the time, that's why he played out in our five-a-side games sometimes and he was very good.

Nobody really had their own spot in the changing room, your peg just depended on what shirt number you were wearing for the game. In those days the numbers were just one to 12 and all the kits would be hung up in order when you got to the changing room. You just got changed where your number was hanging.

- IAN BRITTON
EX-PLAYER 1972-1982

Getting shirty: The kits are lined up on the players' lockers during the 2008-09 season and (left) George Graham prepares beneath his peg in August 1965

PLAYER SUPERSTITIONS

Players were tremendously superstitious in my day and we'd try anything if it helped. But, for me, it was more set routines... like I used to have a kick of the ball in the dressing room.

I'd find an area where I wasn't going to slip up on my backside and just keep the ball moving and feel as though I was loosening up and to get a feel of the ball. But I certainly didn't have to sit in a certain spot and put my left boot on first and so on... I'd gone through all that by the time I was 18!

Believe it or not, there wasn't usually a proper warm-up in our day. Some players wouldn't even run 10 yards in their warm-up!

- BOBBY TAMBLING
EX-PLAYER 1959-1970

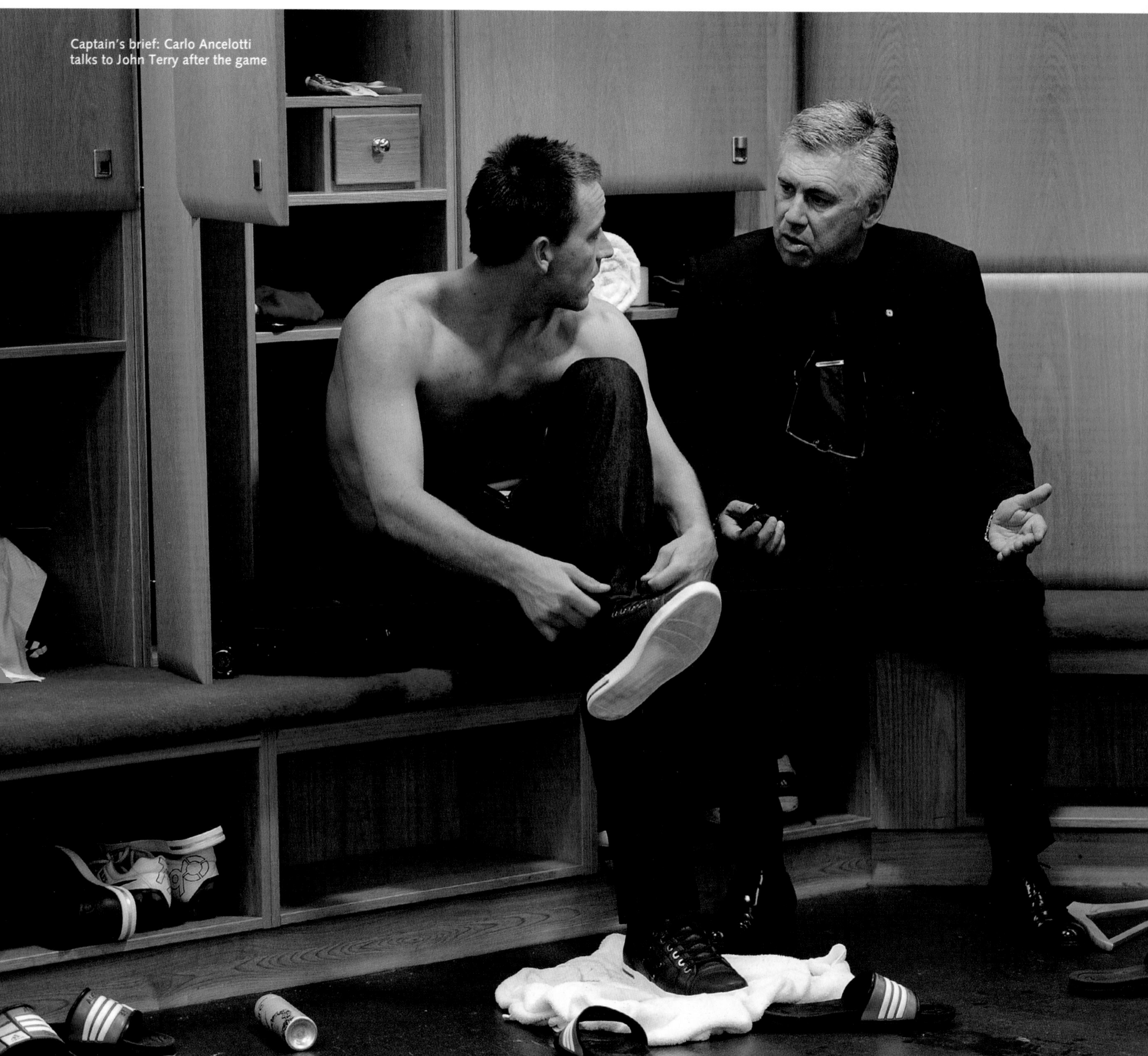

Captain's brief: Carlo Ancelotti talks to John Terry after the game

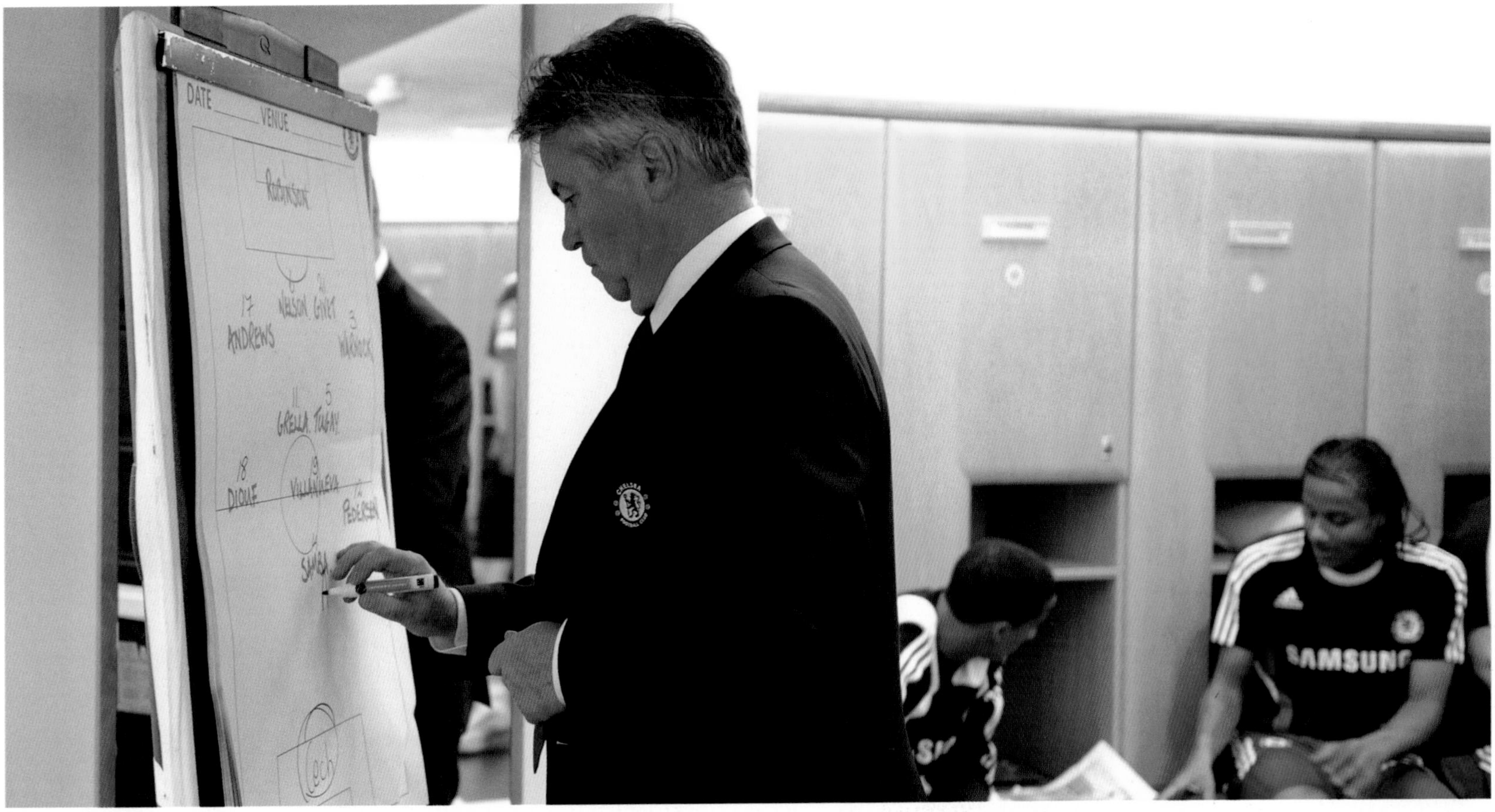

Final preparation: Guus Hiddink works on his tactics, while (below) Carlo Ancelotti congratulates Ramires and Jose Mourinho strides through the dressing room

Men's room: The home dressing room toilets and (left) John Terry and Frank Lampard sign shirts for Huddersfield Town players following their FA Cup meeting in 2008

ROUTINE TOILET VISIT

FRANK LAMPARD: You see everyone doing their little routines – I know JT likes to have a wee on the right-hand side urinal! If I'm standing there and I'm ready to go but I see John coming up, I'll move! You've got to have your captain right for the game!
JOHN TERRY: I have to confirm this. When the dressing room was installed, for some reason I could only go there. And the foreign lads don't really get why I'm waiting behind them when there's spaces elsewhere.

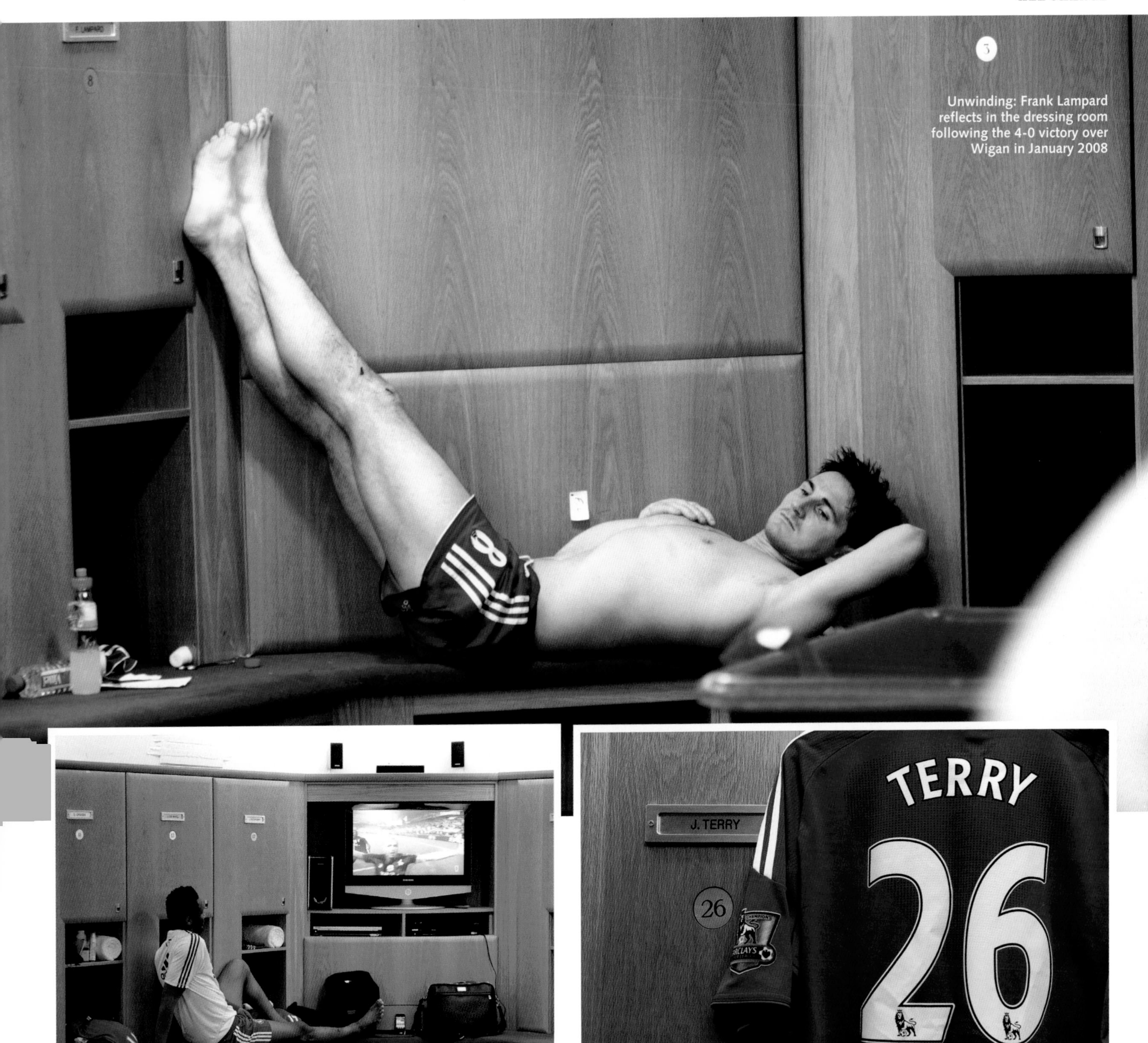

Unwinding: Frank Lampard reflects in the dressing room following the 4-0 victory over Wigan in January 2008

Cleaning up: Micky Droy and Ron Harris return to the dressing room after a muddy match in 1978

PLACE ON THE BENCH

Half the players knew me when I first walked in the dressing room and the other half didn't! I'd only just turned 17... I sat to the right of the entrance and I was up near Roy Bentley and I think on the other side was Peter Sillett.

That became my place in the dressing room, I tried hard to keep it – mainly through superstition. The kit man knew where you liked to sit and would try to make sure he got it in the right place for you.

That first time I walked in the dressing room and saw my shirt... obviously you didn't have the names back then, it was just the number, but it was still unbelievable.

Actually, it was a bit frightening, because the league was still up for grabs and it was everything to play for. So it was a massive game and for a youngster to go into that was very difficult but, to be fair, I had a very good game.

– PETER BRABROOK
EX-PLAYER 1952-1962

In sink: Jose Bosingwa's boots are bathed in hot water to help soften them before kick-off and (right) Marcel Desailly's shirt hangs in the dressing room during the 1999/2000 season

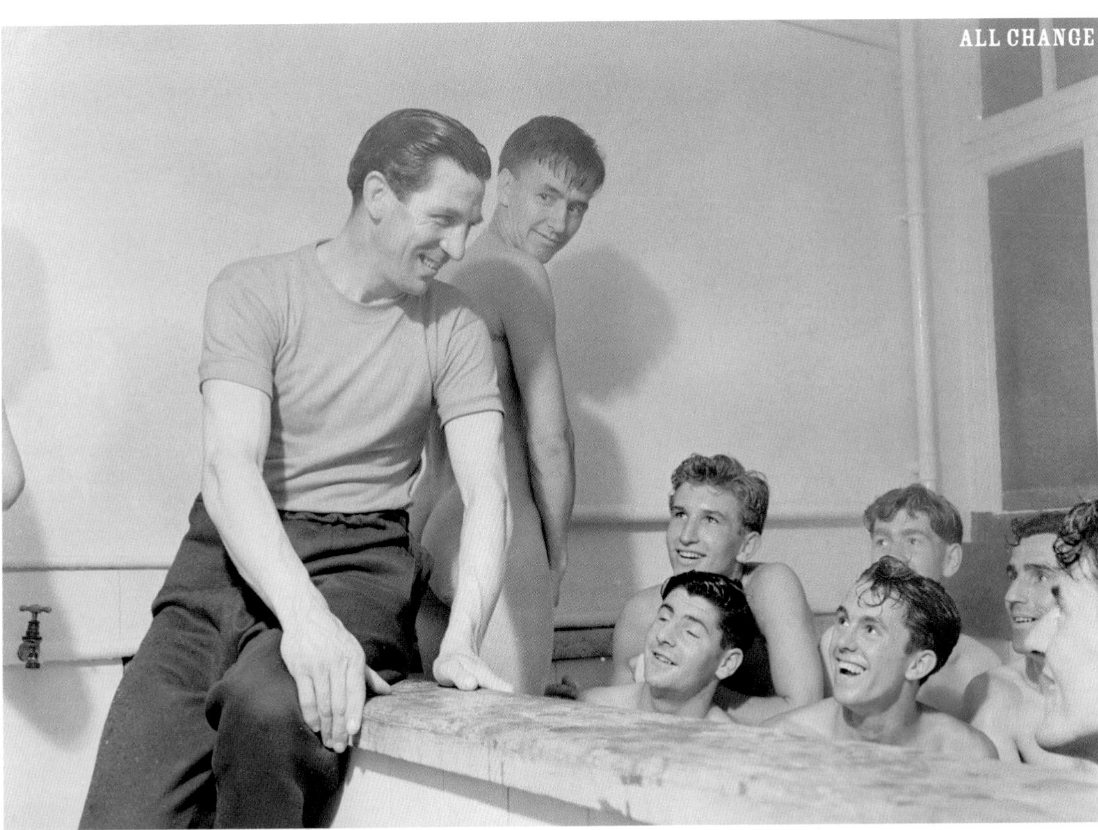

Champagne moment: The team celebrate promotion to the First Division in April 1984 (left); Ted Drake shares a bath-time joke with his players (top) in August 1952; and the home dressing room baths as they looked in 1990

Making their arrival: Didier Drogba and the rest of the Chelsea squad prepare to enter the home dressing room in a relaxed mood

Scoring souvenir: Nicolas Anelka heads home with the matchball after some hat-trick heroics against Sunderland in November 2008

Looking smart: Anelka checks his tie as he prepares to leave Stamford Bridge; Keith Jones and Kerry Dixon get ready for a Division One match in 1986 (bottom)

Prize guys:
Hernan Crespo and
Asier Del Horno
celebrate Chelsea's
first Premiership title
in 2005 along with
team-mates Damien
Duff (top) and Petr
Cech (bottom)

BARCLAYS PREMIERSHIP CHAMPIONS 2004-05
BARCLAYS PREMIERSHIP CHAMPIONS 2004-05
mobile
Vittel
26

Celebration time: John Terry, Didier Drogba and the backrom staff get into the party mood after their 2009/10 title triumph

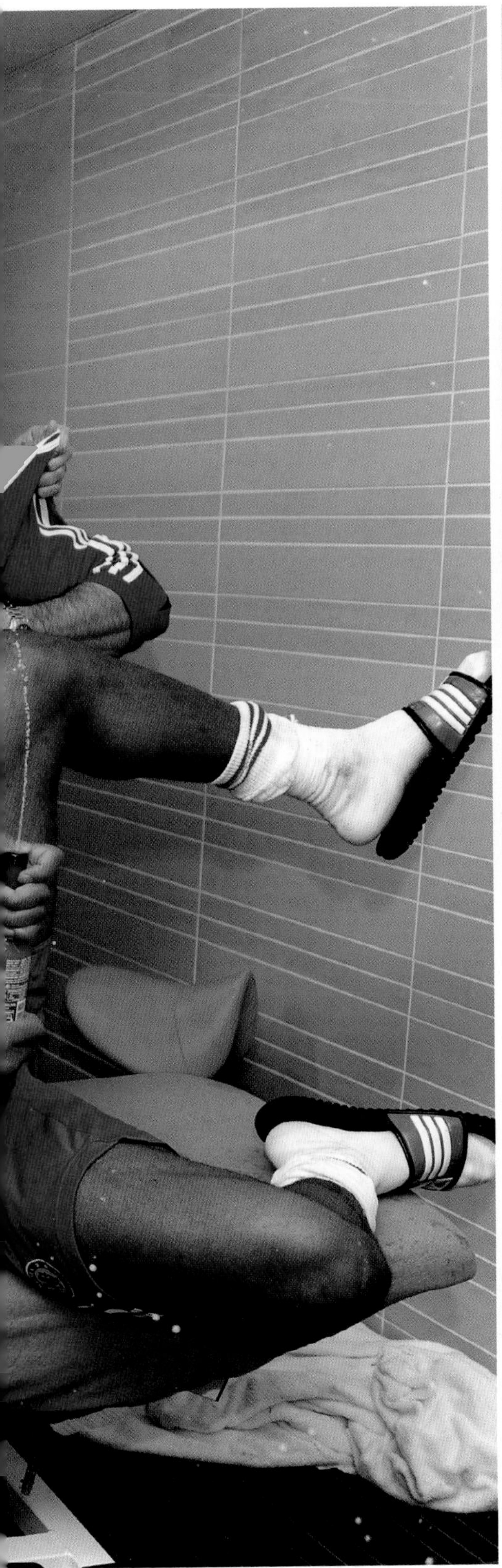

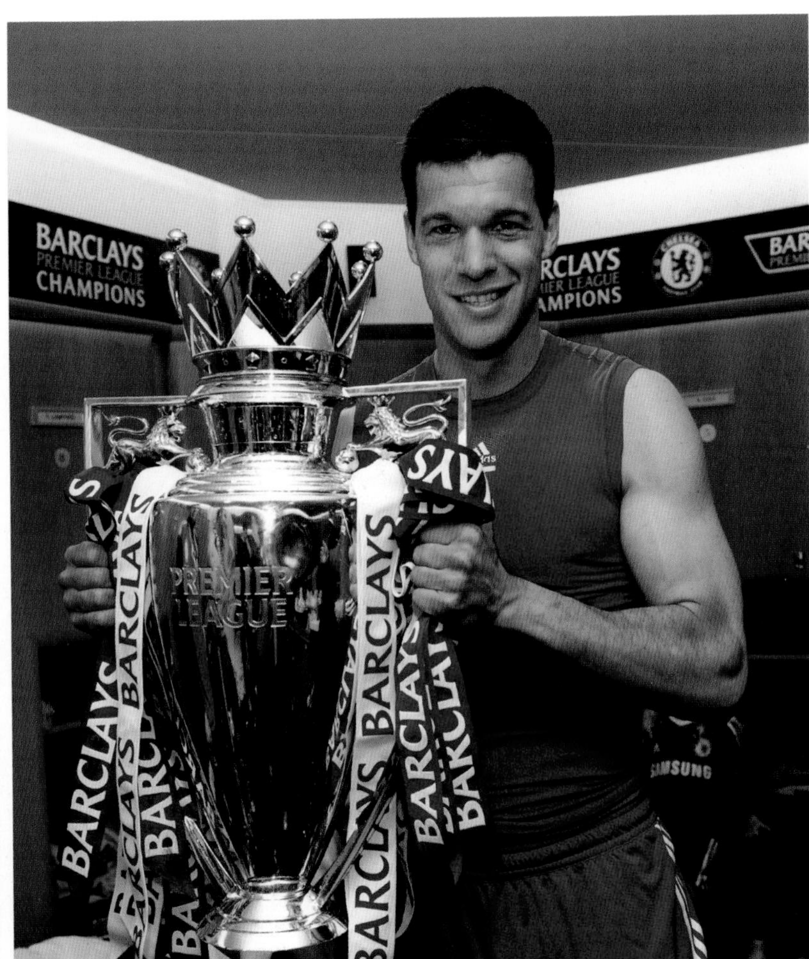

League of their own: Michael Ballack poses with the 2009/10 Premier League trophy in the home dressing room while Didier Drogba sprays some champagne (below)

Three amigos: Didier Drogba, John Terry and Frank Lampard indicate how many Premier League titles they have won (right); Ashley Cole shows off the 2009/10 championship trophy (below); manager Carlo Ancelotti proudly holds their Premier League prize (bottom)

BARCLAYS
BARCLAYS
Vittel

Pre-match checks: Kit man Garry Grey in the boot room ahead of Chelsea's Champions League match with and FC Copenhagen in March 2011

All smiles: Peter Osgood in the Chelsea boot room and (right) with manager Tommy Docherty in 1966, while an injured Alan Hudson swaps his boots for crutches (top left) in 1970

PHYSIO ROOM

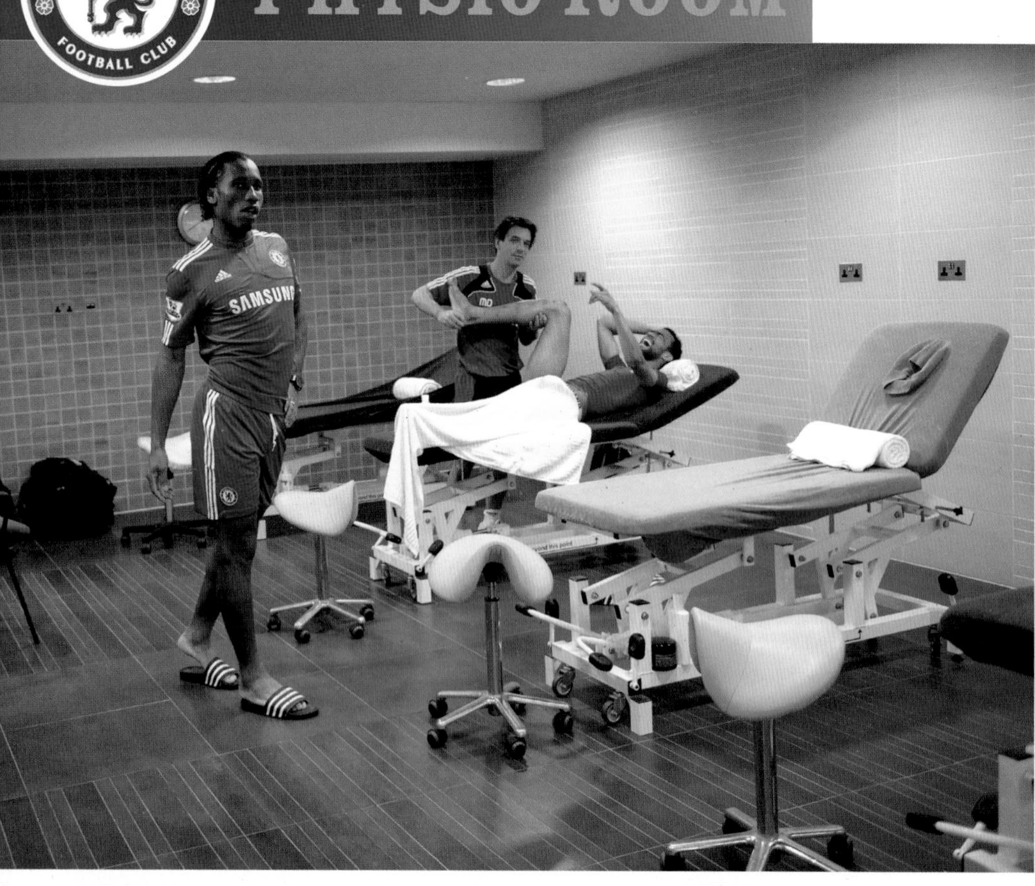

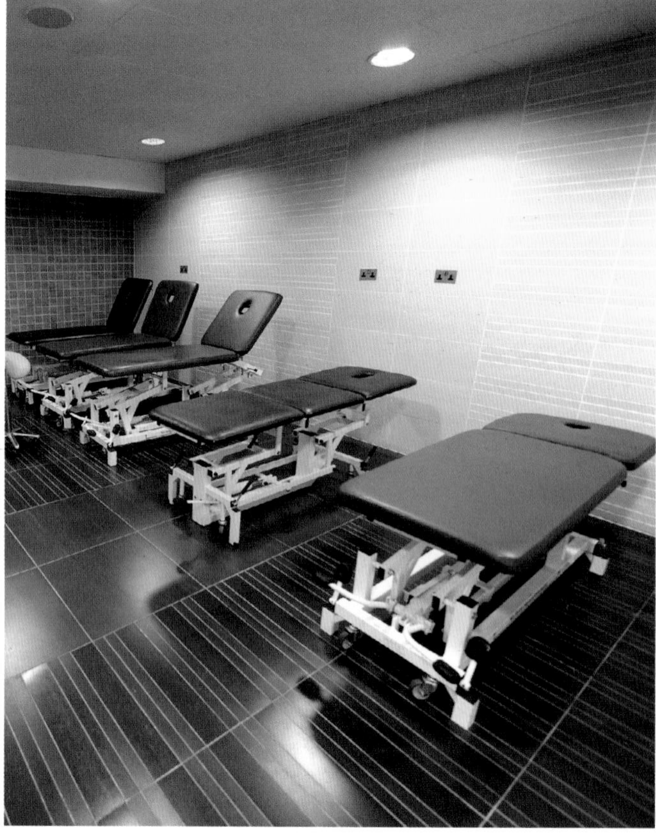

Table toppers: The Stamford Bridge physio facilities and (left) Jose Bosingwa and Mikel get some treatment

NO TIME TO RECOVER

I was sat on the treatment table getting treatment from Harry Medhurst, our trainer, when I was told I'd be making my debut against Southampton.

The news came through that Peter Osgood, Charlie Cooke, Tommy Baldwin and Johnny Boyle were found drunk in a nearby restaurant on the Friday. Believe it or not, it didn't really happen too often. I think they went out for a spot of lunch, but they were a little too close to the ground – it was in Barberella's, which is right next to Stamford Bridge.

In fact, where I was sitting on the treatment table, if the walls were glass I could have seen them knocking the wine back! Not the smartest move, but it was quite funny on the Friday – but not the Saturday.

We got drubbed 5-0, so it wasn't a very good day at the office. I think we were lucky to come away with just five because it could have been double figures.

- ALAN HUDSON
EX-PLAYER 1968-1974 & 1983-1984

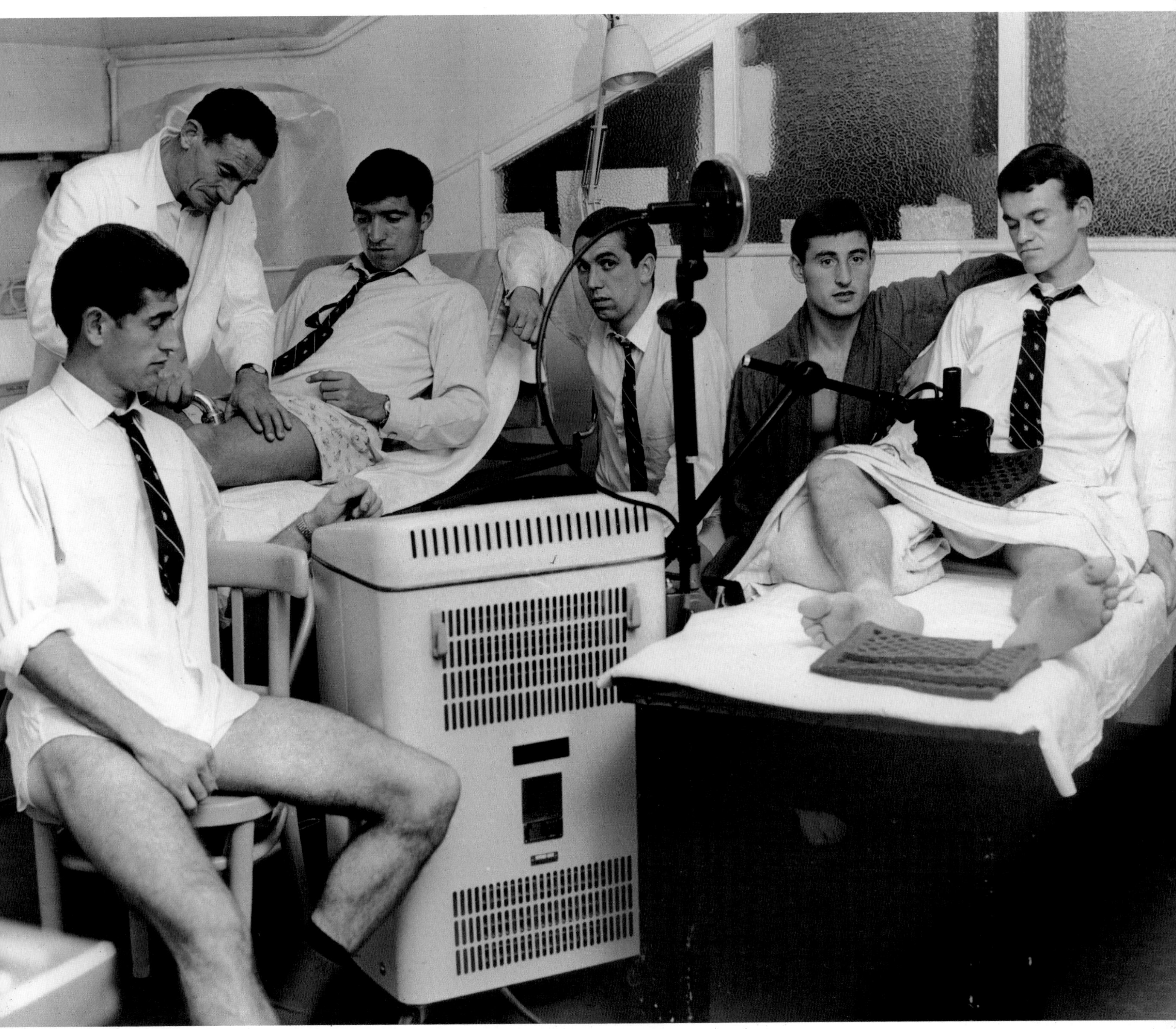

On the mend: (l-r) Peter Bonetti, trainer Harry Medhurst, Terry Venables, Marvin Hinton, Bert Murray and Eddie McCreadie in the treatment room following a Fairs Cup match against Roma in October 1965

MANAGER'S OFFICE

Tactical den: The manager's office at Stamford Bridge and (right) Ted Drake in his office in 1952 and Dave Sexton arrives at work in 1967 (far right)

RECRUITMENT OFFICE

Nowhere particular stands out for me at Stamford Bridge as I had so many good years at Chelsea. I suppose you could say the manager's office as Ted Drake was so good to us. I was 15 and playing for England Schoolboys, and basically had my pick of the clubs to go to.

Ted was always ringing up to see how I was doing. I think Chelsea also knew if they could get me, then Ron would join too. My dad knew that too and I'll never forget his face when I signed for Chelsea. He was an Arsenal fan...

- ALLAN HARRIS
EX-PLAYER 1960-1964
& 1966-1967

REFEREES' ROOM

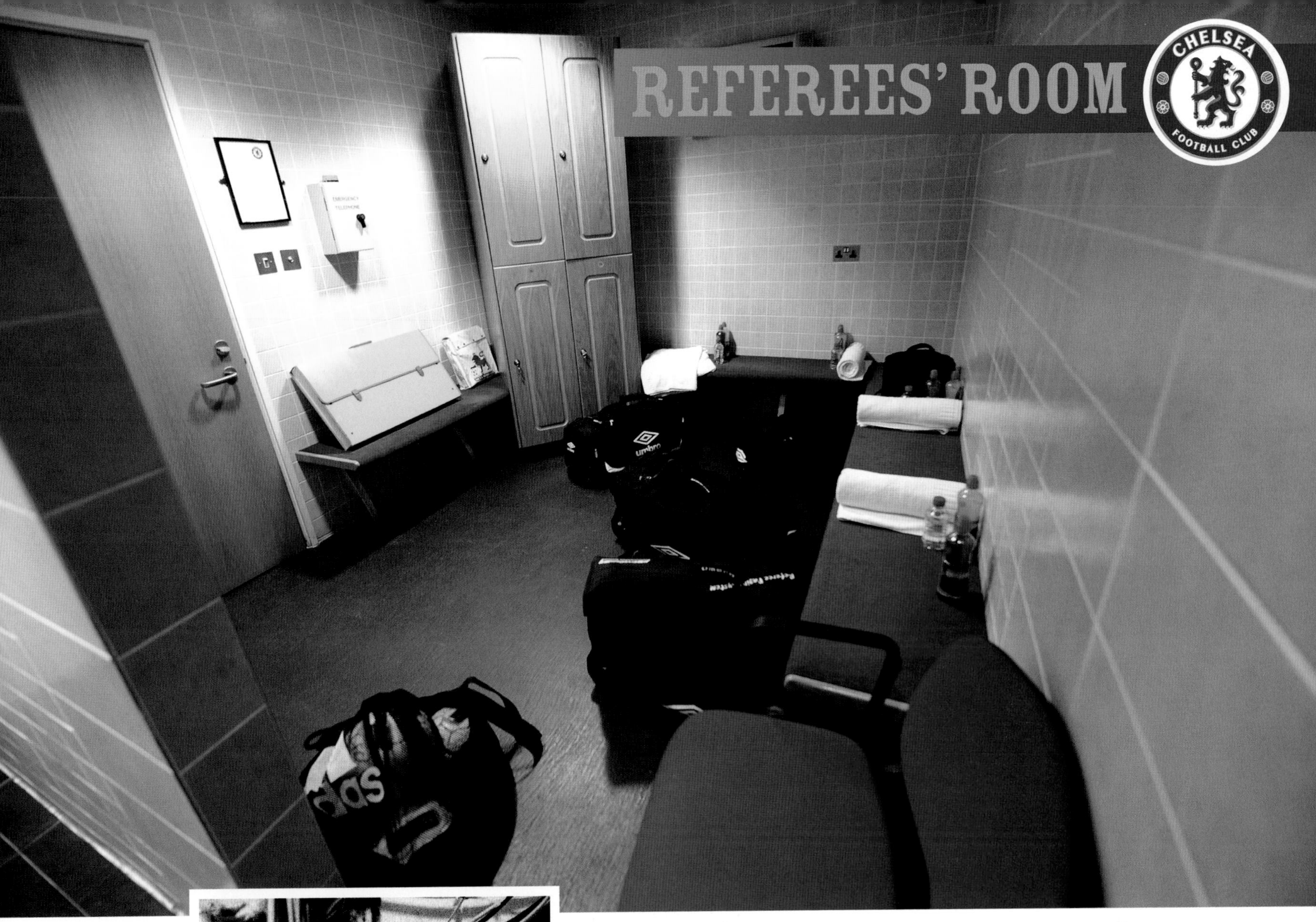

Official residence: The referees' room at Stamford Bridge (above) and old signage in the tunnel (right)

BOOKING IN FOR THE NIGHT

I'd say my favourite part of Stamford Bridge was the room me and Mickey Thomas used to kip in – the referees' room! That was like a second home to Mickey.

Back then, when you signed for a club, they only put you up for a month and in that time you're supposed to move house and find a new place to buy. In a month!

Well, we're two lads from up north and we had no chance of doing that. So when my month had finished, I couldn't find anywhere and I couldn't sell my house up here so I decided to drive every day. I'd leave at 5am, but some days I'd just stay at the Bridge! Mickey was a bit of loose cannon so he'd stay there a lot more than me.

If there was a game, we'd have to find somewhere to get our heads down. I remember sitting outside the Bridge one night with Mickey after we'd played at Brentford in a pre-season game, and we were opposite the Stamford Bridge Arms pub. It was midnight and we said, "Bloody hell, what are we gonna do now?" So we just got in the car and drove home! We had nowhere to stay so we just went home to North Wales.

- JOEY JONES
EX-PLAYER 1982-1985

TUNNEL VISION

The exhilarating feeling you get as you emerge from the depths of the East Stand and onto its hallowed turf is one no player forgets. It's a sight most fondly recalled by the captains who have led the Blues out over the years, but they are all united in the belief that little else compares to the swell of support, generous in their applause, that greets the light at the end of the tunnel...

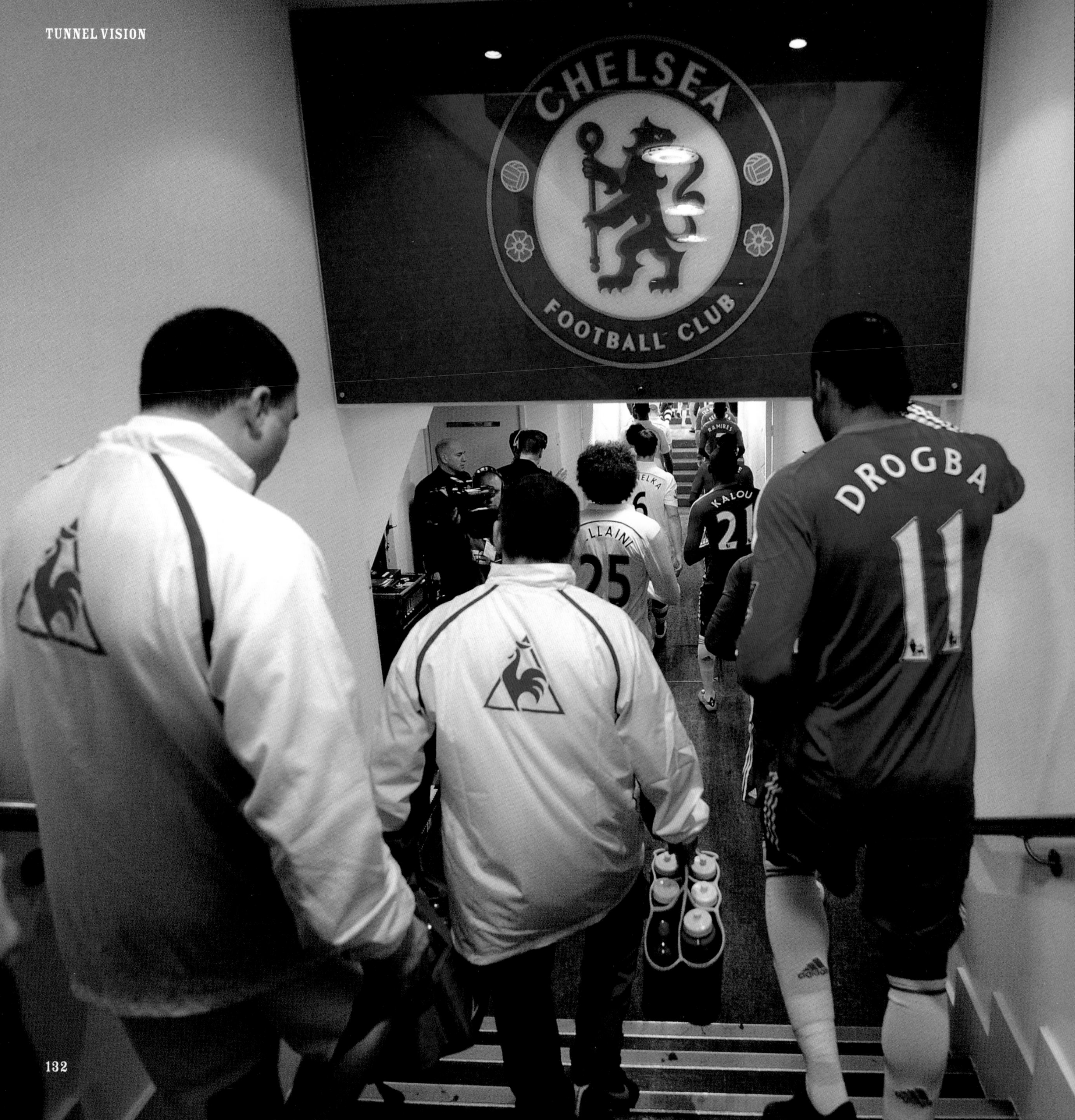
CHELSEA
FOOTBALL CLUB
DROGBA
11
KALOU
21
25

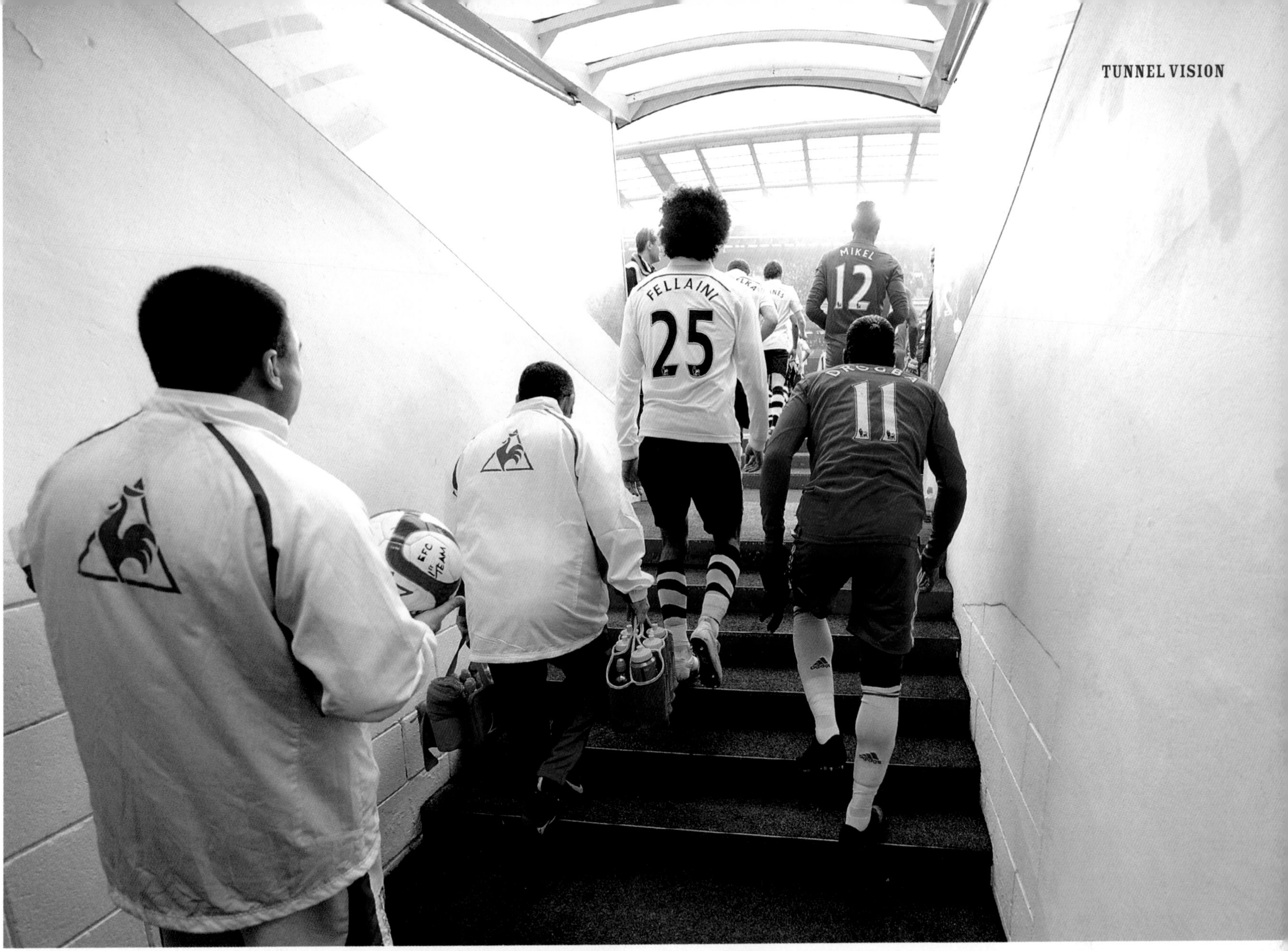

Boot-iful game: The referee conducts last minute boot checks as the players prepare to take to the field

Budweiser
chelseafc.com
UMBRO.COM
SKY SPORTS
KEEP OFF
THE PITCH

AWAY

Well-earned rest:
John Bumstead has a breather in the tunnel after being substituted against Leeds in April 1984

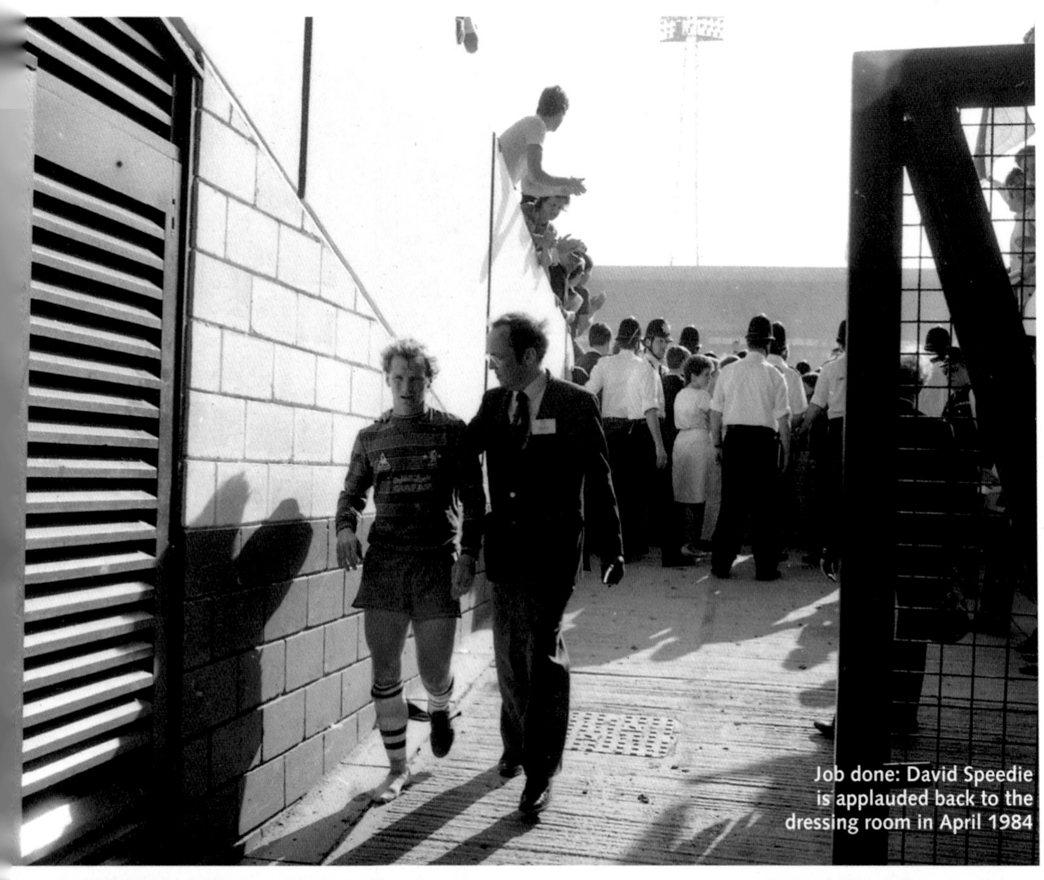

Job done: David Speedie is applauded back to the dressing room in April 1984

GETTING IN THE ZONE

When in the tunnel, I just get in the zone. We've all got little routines that we do, little thought processes that we have and I don't particularly think about the opposition team or any individuals. It's just about myself and us really. Making sure that I'm ready and also making sure everyone else in the line is ready, as captain and vice-captain you try to have a little rally up with the lads and we do that in the tunnel and basically get in the zone.

– FRANK LAMPARD

SPECIAL FEELING

The moment you go out the tunnel and onto the pitch – it's a different feeling, something you would always miss when you finish playing. I love the atmosphere, especially when they sing all the players' names before the game. And if you hear the fans sing your name when you do something good in the game, it's really nice.

- PAULO FERREIRA

CHELSEA FOOTBALL CLUB
chelseafc.com

CHELSEA FOOTBALL CLUB
chelseafc.com
chelseafc.com

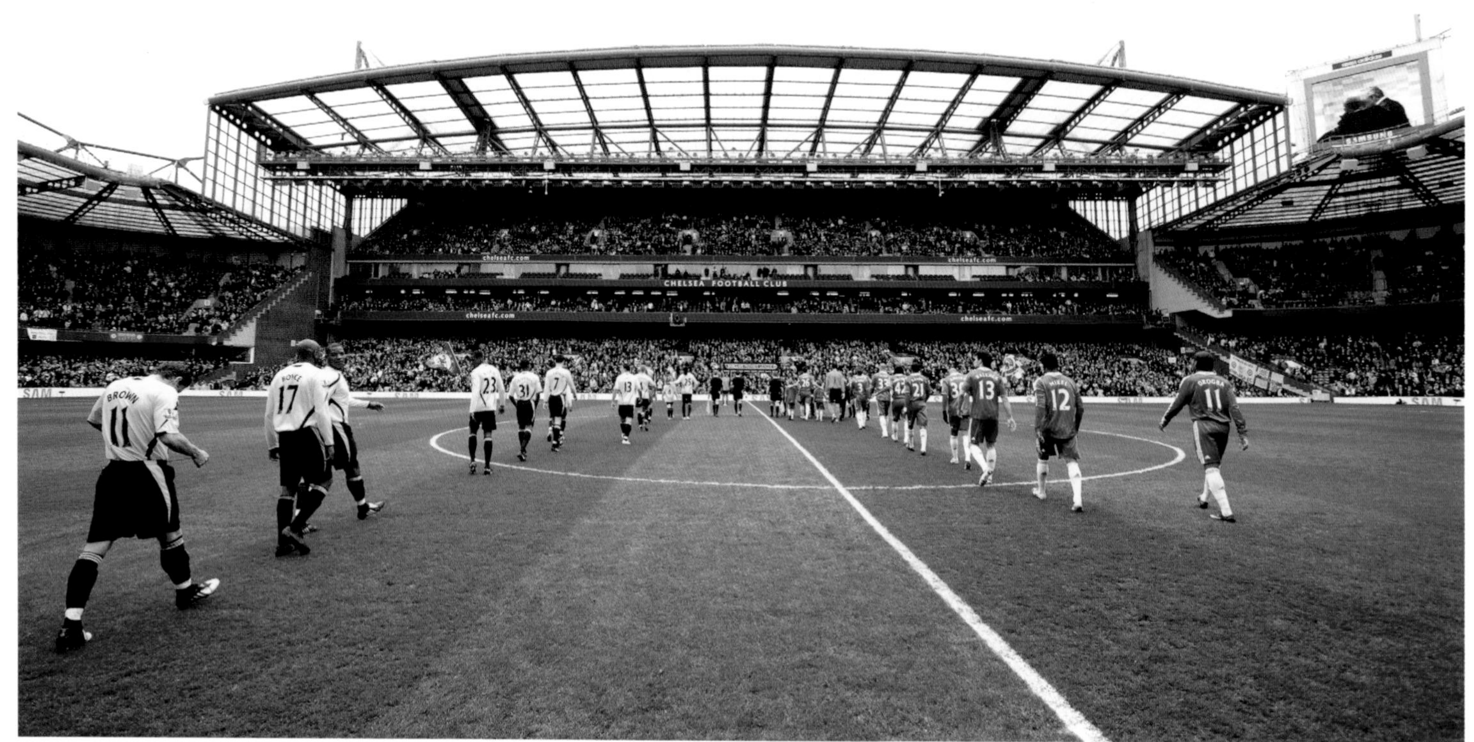

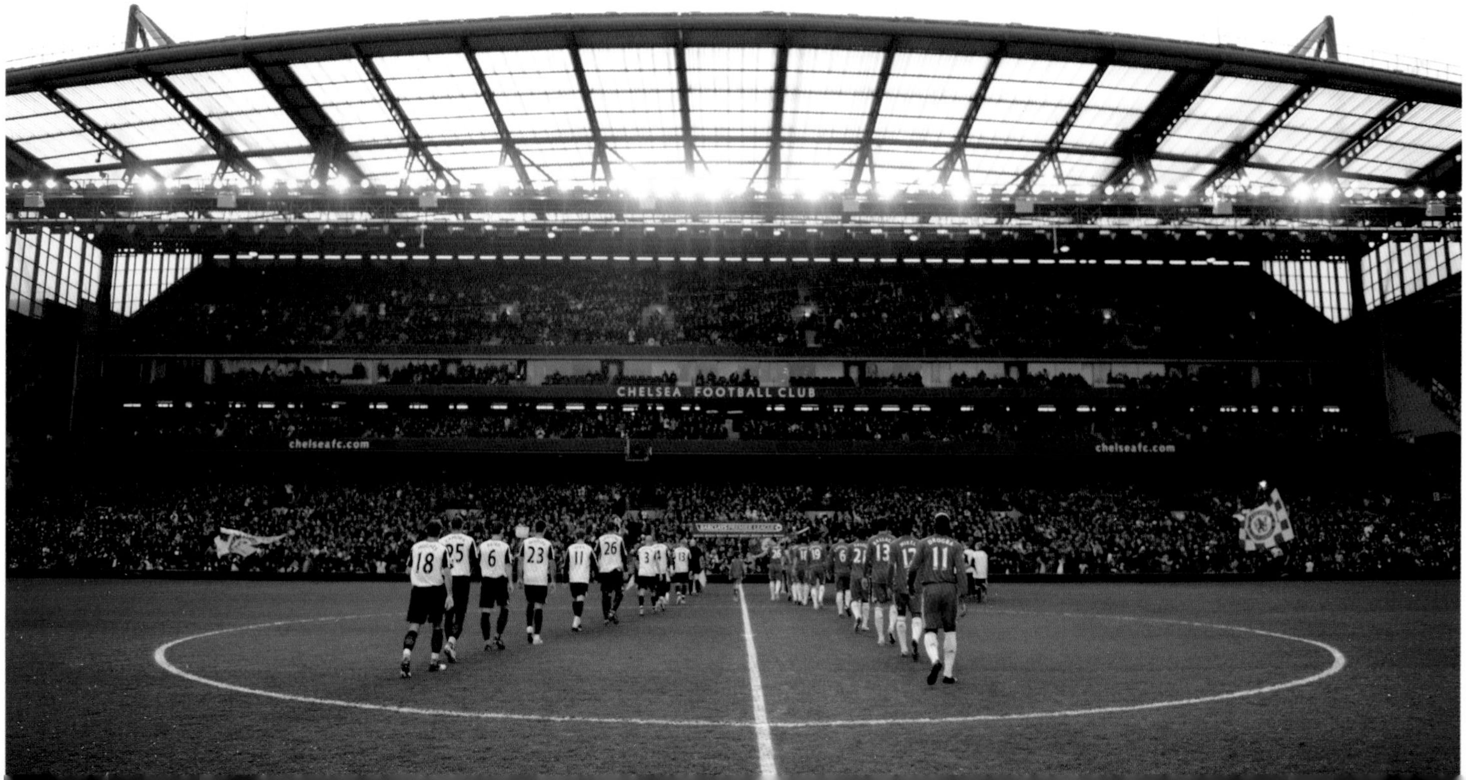

Leading the way: (clockwise from top left) Players emerge during the 1939/40 season; Ron Harris leads his side out against Birmingham in January 1970; Jimmy Greaves is cheered onto the pitch during his final Chelsea appearance in April 1961 – a 4-3 win over Nottingham Forest in which he scored all four of the Blues' goals; while Micky Droy and Gary Locke take to the field for the FA Cup fifth round match against Crystal Palace in February 1976

Treading the boards: Jimmy Greaves runs out to the sacred soil of Stamford Bridge in 1960

View from the sidelines: Carlo Ancelotti stands in the home dugout next to his backroom staff during the Premier League encounter with Manchester United in March 2011, while (below right) Jose Mourinho watches his side in Champions League action in 2005

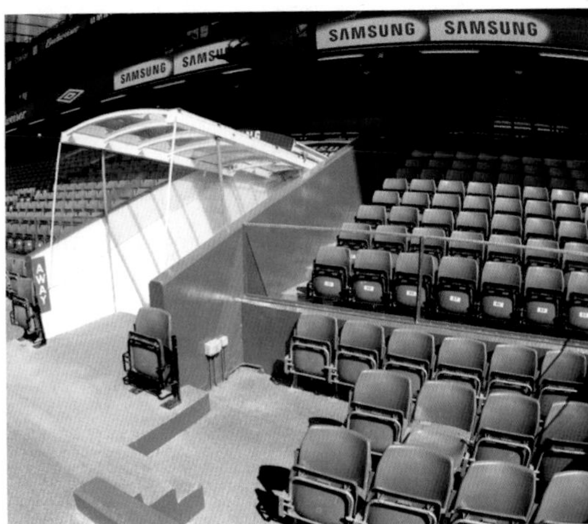

Viewing area: The dugouts at Stamford Bridge during the 1985/86 campaign

Proud display: Club trophy cabinets located in the museum

Prize joker: Chelsea's Chris Hutchings fools around in the club Trophy Room in 1981

From small beginnings: Exhibits at the old Chelsea Museum as visitors take a tour of the club's history

Model professionals: Frank Lampard and John Terry's waxworks on show at the museum in 2005 along with some prized Gianfranco Zola paraphernalia (below)

Proud moment: Mickey Thomas takes his applause from the fans in the Directors' Box after promotion in 1984, while Eddie Niedzwiecki and Joey Jones share a celebratory hug (below)

Crowd salute: Colin Lee and Joe McLaughlin in the Directors' Box after securing promotion to the First Division with a 5-0 victory over Leeds United on April 28, 1984

CHELSEA VIP

From the Directors' Box to the Players' Lounge, some areas of Stamford Bridge remain exclusive to a select few. As well as hosting numerous dignitaries, however, they have been a focal point for some unrestricted celebrations...

Title speech: Chelsea manager Ted Drake addresses the fans from the Directors' Box after securing the First Division championship for the first time in 1955

Players' Bar: David Speedie and John Bumstead enjoy some post-match refreshment while Mickey Thomas (left) raises a glass in celebration after securing promotion in April 1984

Fashionable place: The Directors' Lounge in the West Stand, known as the Dolce & Gabbana Lounge

Host with the most: Ron Harris entertains guests in an East Stand Executive Box as part of his matchday hospitality duties

Speaking Frankly: Kerry Dixon chats to Frank Lampard in a Millennium Box and (right) the matchday hospitality experience

HOSPITALITY SUITES

I do the matchday hospitality with Peter Bonetti and we both really look forward to it. A large part of my life revolves around Chelsea and we're all exceptionally well treated by the club when we turn up on matchdays.

Things have changed for the better around the club in terms of the way they treat us former players and it would be upsetting not to be recognised.

Now there's the Harris Suite and the Bonetti Suite and I was chuffed about that because we played more than 1,500 games for the club between us.

It's really nice to turn up, see Roman Abramovich, and the first thing he does is come over to shake me by the hand.

- RON HARRIS
EX-PLAYER 1961-1980

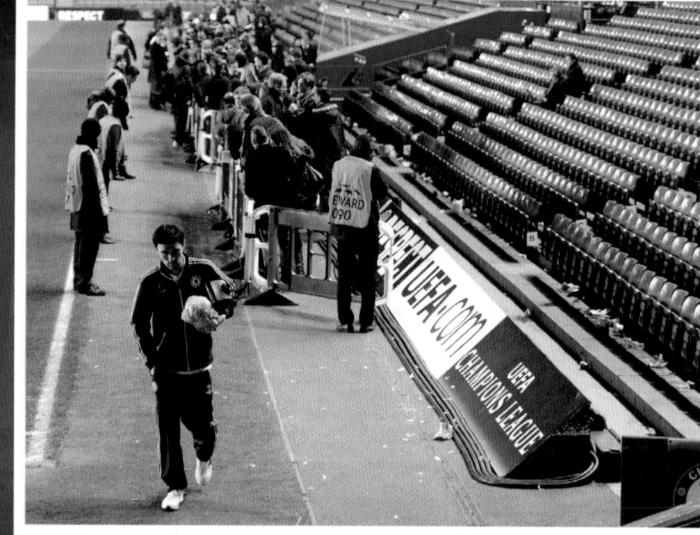

Media scramble: Branislav Ivanovic conducts an interview (left) while Michael Essien (below) heads home and Yuri Zhirkov passes the media mixed zone following a Champions League game (top)

QUIET OFF THE PITCH

Off the pitch, I'm a quiet person. I don't really like talking or doing interviews, but when I'm on the pitch, that's a different thing altogether.

The pitch is like my office and when you're in the office, you don't mess around – you mean business.

– MICHAEL ESSIEN

Press conference:
Carlo Ancelotti
addresses the media

Host team: Scott Minto and Jason Cundy in their presenting roles on Chelsea TV

Interview: Chelsea TV's Jason Cundy interviews Ashley Cole at a Player of the Year dinner and (left) the studio and gallery

FAN, PLAYER AND PRESENTER

The first time I went to Stamford Bridge I was six and now I'm 41, so I've been involved with the club for the last 35 years. I signed with the club as a schoolboy at the age of 11 and went on to play for them and now I work for them on the media side of things.

Now, when I'm working at game, I still walk up those steps in the East Stand and get exactly the same feeling I did all those years ago when I see the pitch.

The football may have changed a lot but it's the same club I grew up supporting, it's got the same feel and it's like a family to me.

- JASON CUNDY
EX-PLAYER 1988 1992

Press pack: Journalists watch the action unfold from the Press Box and (below right) a steward holds up the attendance figure for the media

Talking a good game: The view from the commentary box in the East Stand

INTENSE EXPERIENCE

I thought this training session was a bit short compared to ours. It was short but it was amazing to see how good the players are, how good as athletes they are and how they train.

Soccer is similar a little bit. You guys obviously use your feet but it is high intensity, moving around a lot, reacting. My son enjoys playing it. I also got to speak with John Terry, Michael Essien and Didier Drogba. Sportsmen always have something they can talk about.

- STEVE SMITH
CAROLINA PANTHERS NFL STAR

WHITBREAD
OXO

Jump to it: The Chelsea squad are put through their paces at Stamford Bridge in 1939

TRAINING AT THE BRIDGE

We didn't train at Stamford Bridge very often. We used to train at the training ground, but one day a week, usually on a Friday, we used to do a few sprints and play behind the goal at Stamford Bridge. Then we'd go on the pitch to do a few set-plays and things like that. But it wasn't that often we got to go on the pitch at Chelsea.

- RON HARRIS
EX-PLAYER 1961-1980

Warming up: Chelsea's 1980 squad train in front of the old Shed

FIVE-A-SIDE IN FRONT OF THE SHED

During my time as an apprentice, we used to train behind the goal at the Shed End. There was an area of pitch behind the goal before the greyhound track, so if ever we couldn't go to the training ground and had to train at the Bridge, we'd have five-a-side competitions there.

It could be pretty intense at times, but it was a bit surreal – you've got this pitch you were desperate to play on, but you weren't allowed to because it was for the first team. It was a taster of what you could get.

I think it was a couple of years after doing this for the first time that I actually made my Chelsea debut.

So those five-a-side games could have been as near as I ever got to the pitch!

I remember having to run up and down the stands. You were launching yourself up the East Stand, which was like going up the sheer face of a mountain because it was so steep!

So you looked forward to training at the Bridge because of the five-a-side games, but at the same time you hated it because you were either doing that or doing laps of the greyhound track before you got to the good bit.

– GRAHAM STUART
EX-PLAYER 1989-1993

CELEBRATION TIME

Stamford Bridge has witnessed plenty of success in recent seasons, so it's only natural the players are well versed in the art of celebration. From strange goalscoring routines to traditional cup raising, the Chelsea squad have raised the standard...

Roar passion: John Terry holds aloft the 2004/05 Premiership trophy and (right) Carlo Cudicini takes in the atmosphere along with Petr Cech and Didier Drogba (far right)

ENDING THE 50-YEAR TITLE WAIT

I will always remember the atmosphere when we won the title during the last home game of the 2004/05 season against Charlton. People had been waiting for it for 50 years and you could see at the beginning of the game there were some adults who were long-term fans, guys with all the tattoos and flags and things... they were crying! So this was something amazing.

It was a brilliant season because when I signed the contract with the club and was told I was the first-choice keeper, there was a lot of pressure.

The supporters had always been loving Carlo Cudicini, it was very difficult for me. I had to be spot-on in every game to win over everybody, so the satisfaction at the end was huge.

– PETR CECH

A SEASON TO BE PROUD OF

My favourite moment at Stamford Bridge is winning the title in 2005, definitely. After 50 years, we finally won the league again. I had come to a different club at the start of that season, a different country and a different kind of football. So to lift the title at Stamford Bridge in my first year was just a fantastic moment – my favourite memory of the place.

– PAULO FERREIRA

Memorable occasion: Paulo Ferreira shows the league trophy off to the fans in May 2005 and the team celebrate alongside manager Jose Mourinho (below)

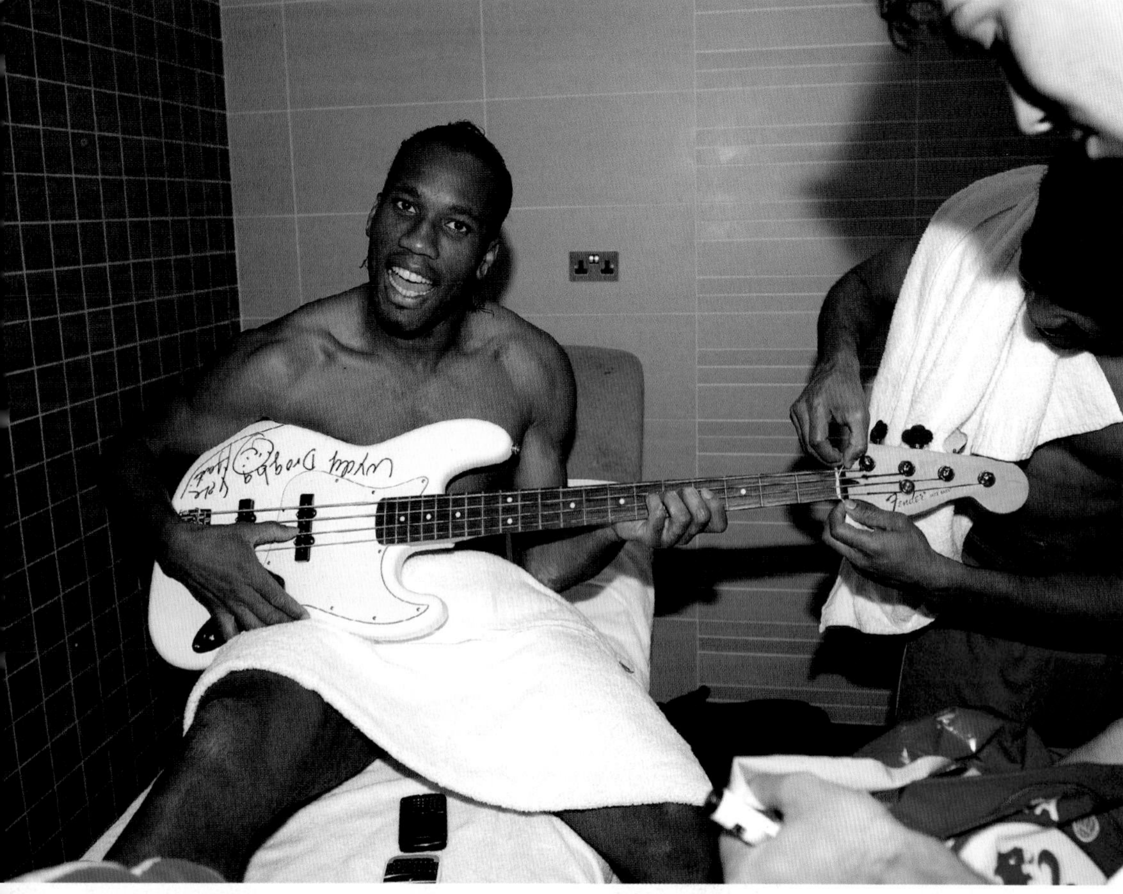

Ace of the bass: Dider Drogba with the guitar given to him by Wyclef Jean and (below) taking his prized possession home

GUITAR HERO

This celebration came at the end of a wonderful season for us. Didier was really happy because he was scoring and competing for the Golden Boot and you can feel happiness and satisfaction on our faces. We want to live that again.

Me and Didier want to start a band, that's true. I've been taking drumming lessons for over a year now. I'm improving, but the next step for me is to play in a band. I like to go to watch gigs, live shows, I'm always backstage because I like to see and get that experience. I don't know if I'll do it soon, but I'll try. And Didier got a bass guitar from Wyclef Jean, so he said he'll start to learn because he likes music too.

My drumming is going well, I really like it. You can say it's a hobby, a new passion, but I always liked drums. I just never had the opportunity to start. Now I have so I have my drums at home and every day I'm practising. But I don't drive my wife crazy because it's electronic, so I have the headphones on – so no noise!

– FLORENT MALOUDA

BRINGING TEAMS TO THEIR KNEES

Here I am sliding to celebrate in front of Rafa Benitez. It wasn't meant to be me saying: "Don't speak too soon" but he had made some comments that were not justified before we played Liverpool in the Champions League semi-final in 2008.

He didn't know that, by making those comments, he gave me a lot of confidence and motivation. When something hurts or something wrong is said, the truth always comes out, there is always justice.

When I scored, I dived in front of the fans – just for him – but, after I did that, I realised: 'No, I have to go and celebrate in front of the bench.' It was a big game, an important game and I scored two important goals.

Only a few days before we were all at Lampsy's mum's funeral and it was a hard week for us – a very difficult week – but we went to the final with this win and I wish we can enjoy this kind of moment again soon.

– DIDIER DROGBA

SUPPORTERS ON SONG

There is a photo of me going to the stand after lifting the Premier League trophy in 2006. I'm looking at the supporters because it was the first time I heard them sing: "Didier Drogba, la la la la la!" I was shocked because this is a song that took me back to my days in Marseille, where they used to sing it for me. It was a really special day for us and to hear this being sung was really quite amazing.

- DIDIER DROGBA

CELEBRATORY KISS

We won 3-0 against Manchester United and after the third goal from Riccy (Carvalho), we did a celebration that was a special kind of kiss, from an African song that we have in the Ivory Coast, but a lot of people thought we were trying to mime cigars.

We've shared a lot of fantastic moments together at this club – all the people here – and that's why I call this a family, it's just like that around here.

- DIDIER DROGBA

REFLECTING BACK

I see this picture a lot as it's up in one of the corridors at the training ground – it always makes me smile when I see it.

I was using the Premier League trophy as my mirror, making sure I look good for the pictures!

When I was a kid, all I wanted to do was play football and come to the Premier League. And to win it, of course!

It was a fantastic day and a great way to end my first season in English football. To do it with a 3-0 win over Man United just made it even more special.

– MICHAEL ESSIEN

BARCA THUNDERBOLT

This is a great picture of my goal against Barcelona in 2009. I think this is definitely one of the best goals I've ever scored. It was such a great moment, one of the greatest in my football career.

I just saw the ball coming down and the only thing that came into my mind was to try and shoot. And it was with my left foot!

At first I was not too sure it was in because it hit the bar first, but then I saw it in the back of the net and that was such a great feeling. I was so happy, I can't really explain how I felt at that time.

– MICHAEL ESSIEN

ARMED FORCE

This goal meant so much to me, and my celebration [thumping his lower arm] was what we call in Brazil "superacao". The word literally translates to "overcome" in English. It's like persistence, but it's something more – like winning a race when you didn't look like you would, we have mental and physical strength and we say "superacao!" and do this with our arms.

- JULIANO BELLETTI
EX-PLAYER 2007-2010

CHELSEA
FOOTBALL CLUB
15
chelseafc.com
e-on

Six of the best: Peter Osgood, Marvin Hinton, Barry Bridges, Terry Venables, John Hollins and goalkeeper Peter Bonetti pose at Stamford Bridge in 1966

Big kick: The ball is launched upfield during Chelsea's encounter with Arsenal at Stamford Bridge in February 1937

Final farewell: Jimmy Greaves takes in the atmosphere ahead of his last game for Chelsea in 1961 and (below) the match ball is tested

WHOLE NEW BALL GAME

Stamford Bridge has been the home of Chelsea Football Club since the turn of the Twentieth Century, but over the decades it has also provided an arena for other sports and organisations. From international football to greyhounds, cricket to cycling, the hallowed turf has been in popular demand...

At the crease: Ian Botham batting for Somerset in the Lambert & Butler cricket competition at Stamford Bridge in 1982, and (right) Graham Gooch looks for the boundary

MOVING THE BOUNDARIES

I remember Chelsea actually hosting some cricket at the Bridge. There might have been a few crowd killers with the boundaries they had, especially with Ian Botham out there! Football pitches just aren't big enough for cricket, though. But I'd still like to have given it a go – it would have been good fun and I could have got my average up.

– GRAHAM THORPE
FORMER CRICKETER

Light relief: The West Indies cricket team try to catch out Geoff Hurst before taking on Essex at Stamford Bridge (below) in Britain's first floodlit cricket match in August 1980

Let's play ball: A member of the Oxford University baseball team takes a swing as they bat against Chelsea at Stamford Bridge in May 1925; Chelsea baseball player Charlie Brookes warming up for the innings (below left); and Prince Albert, The Duke of York, greets the New York Giants before their game against the Chicago White Sox at Stamford Bridge in October 1924

Over the bar: B H Baker on his way to winning the high jump event at the AAA Championships at Stamford Bridge on June 22, 1912; D C Bailey winning the veterans 100 yards handicap at the City of London Police Athletics meeting August 6, 1929 (below left); and I Barnett takes a 'shot' at Stamford Bridge during the 1911 AAA Championships (below right)

Loading up: Dogs are put in the traps at Stamford Bridge in June 1950; the old results board behind the stands (bottom right); and Peter Brabrook in his Chelsea playing days in November 1955 (below)

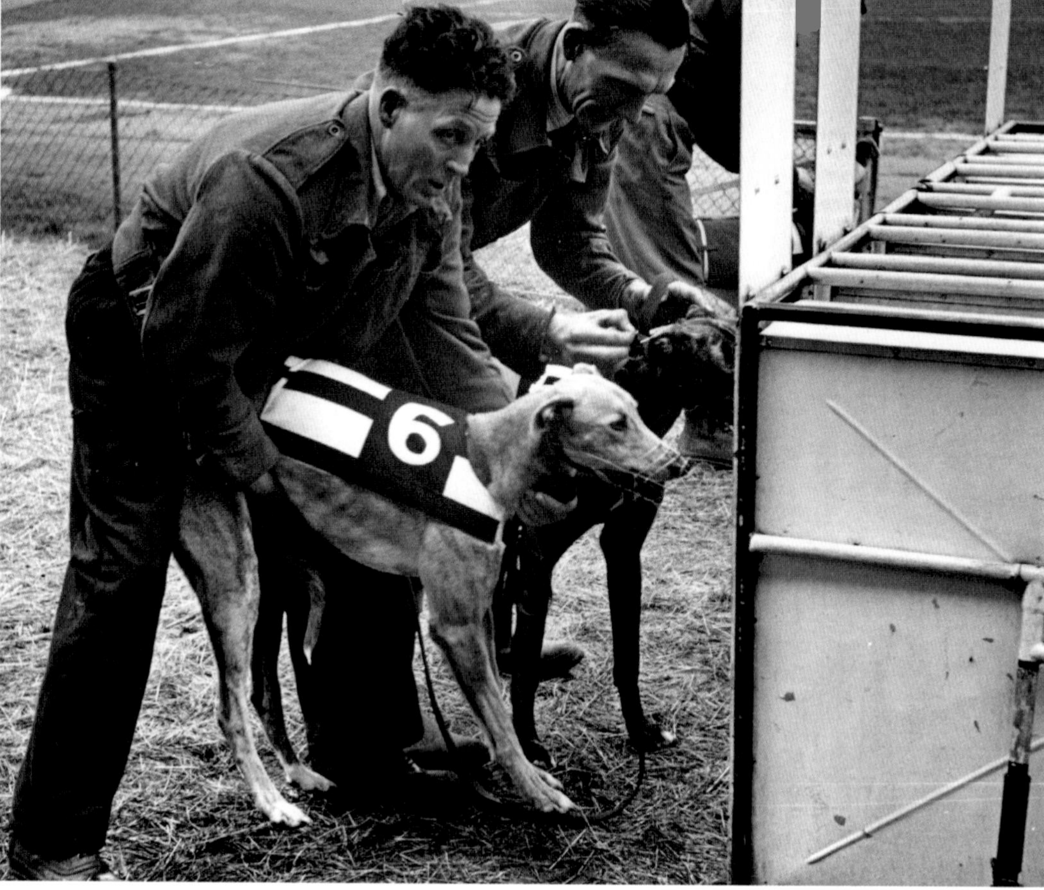

GONE TO THE DOGS

I've got loads of marvellous memories from the year we won the league in 1955. I think the actual pitch itself stands out – it's hard to describe how I felt when I first ran on it in a Chelsea shirt.

Then there was the greyhound track around the pitch, which was unique at the time. They used to have racing there on a Thursday and on a Saturday night if we were at home.

I didn't go to see the races in the evening, but I'd go to the trials because they were in the morning and sometimes we'd be training at the Bridge. We'd finish training and then they'd get started, so I'd stick around to watch it.

I always hoped I'd get some decent tips there and then I could make a few quid, but it never happened – I think I always got the wrong tip! I never had any winners.

- PETER BRABROOK
EX-PLAYER 1954-1962

In the lead: A handler gets the greyhounds ready for a trial race at Stamford Bridge in June 1950

Race fan: Frank Blunstone in 1954

OTHER SIDE OF THE TRACK

One of my favourite memories is the old greyhound track. It was unique in that not many grounds had one.

I'd go and watch the greyhound races from time to time, but we weren't supposed to. The lads used to nick on every now and again. The manager didn't want us gambling, we were banned!

I can't remember any good wins, but we had a maximum wage in those days so we didn't have much to bet with – we couldn't afford to put bets on!

The other good thing about it is that it got us out of training on a Monday morning! We had no training ground so we were at Stamford Bridge and the whistle used to blow at 11 o'clock and we'd have to come off because the dog track went on.

Could you imagine that happening now? They could have got the dogs to chase us, it would have been a good bit of fitness training!

- FRANK BLUNSTONE
EX-PLAYER 1953-1964

Lions' den: England players take time out during a training session at Stamford Bridge prior to their match against Wales in the British Home Championship tournament played throughout the 1959/60 season

International duty: The Charlton brothers, Jack and Bobby, at Stamford Bridge prior to the Home International against Scotland in April 1965 while England take on Italy in January 1955 (below)

On yer bike: Dirt track riders W Banner and F Cooper at Stamford Bridge, once the home to speedway, and (right) professional cyclists speed around the track

Sing when you're wining: Accent perform for the crowd prior to kick-off

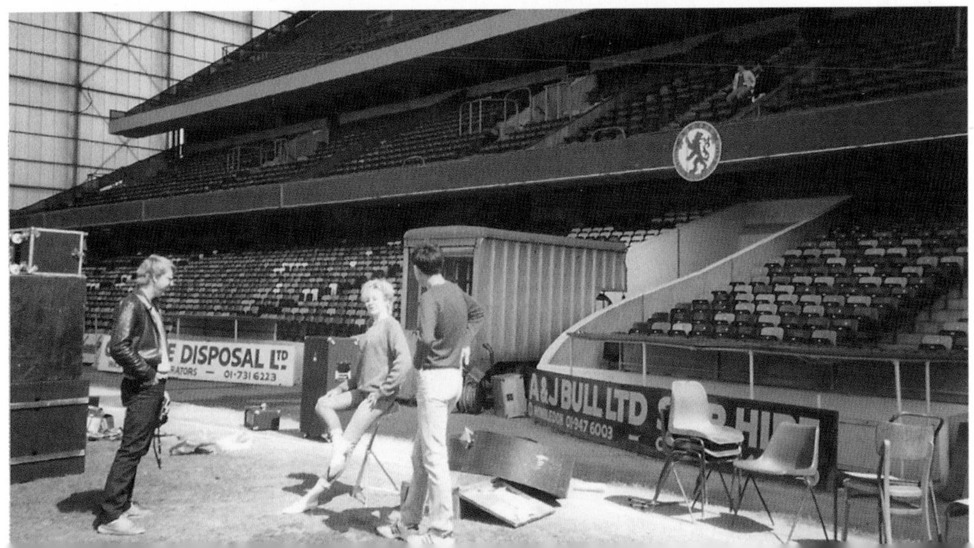

ACCENT TO STARDOM

We walked into reception and the secretary was there. Ken Bates' office was through there and we just said: "We're in a band, can we play on the pitch before the game."

I think Ken Bates overheard it and just said: "Yeah, all right, fine, have a word with the secretary and she'll take all your details..."

It was really low key, very casual. We just brought the van up, unloaded the gear in the tunnel where the players came out and we set up before the game.

- MICK ROBINSON
ACCENT BASSIST

CELEBRITY HANG-OUT

The Blues have a huge following in celebrity circles. From Hollywood movie stars to sporting heavyweights, presenters to politicians and musicians to magicians, there's been a whole array of famous faces at Stamford Bridge over the years...

Acting legend: Chelsea Life President Sir Richard Attenborough with his personalised shirt (above) and greeting John Terry in the stands (left)

In the frame: Famed photographer Terry O'Neill outside the Shed End and (right) Raquel Welch pictured in the Chelsea kit

INTRODUCING SOME WELCH CULTURE

I was working with Raquel Welch in Spain on a film and she knew I was mad about Chelsea because every weekend I'd be trying to find out what the score was. Anyway, I had the idea of dressing her up in Peter Osgood's shirt – I just thought it would cause a bit of a stir.

So I did the picture and then she was driving me mad about meeting Ossie, so I brought her down to Chelsea the next season.

We got to Stamford Bridge and we had to walk right in front of the Shed to get to our seats – everyone was whistling and shouting when they saw who it was.

Raquel loved it. And then she met all the guys, including Ossie. I think it made his day!

I can remember reading in a previous edition of Chelsea magazine that Jimmy Hill claimed he took Raquel to the match, but that's nonsense. He did meet her, but I was the one who took her along to the game.

– TERRY O'NEILL

Causing a stir: Raquel Welch gets animated as she takes in a Chelsea match alongside Jimmy Hill

Entertainers: Music mogul William Orbit stands in an empty Stamford Bridge and (below) singer Damon Albarn spotted in the crowd

ATMOSPHERE MAKES A BIG DIFFERENCE

It seems really weird to be here in the stadium when it's empty, it's amazing how different it feels. I'm fascinated by the difference sound makes to the atmosphere of places, it's what I look at when I'm planning a performance somewhere, and it really is quite eerie being the only one here.

I've only ever been here during a game before, when it's full and there's lots of noise, so to see it empty is almost overwhelming. It has such a different affect on you, you can really feel a sense of the size of the stadium, it seems so much smaller when everyone's packed into the stands.

Also, when you're looking down at the pitch, you don't realise how high you are. Down on the pitch this must be what it's like for the players, with the stands towering above you.

– WILLIAM ORBIT

GRAND DAY OUT TURNED INTO LONG LOVE AFFAIR

The first game I ever went to was an England match and then I asked my dad to take us to a league match. I supported Chelsea and my brother supported Spurs, so he took us to Watford!

But when I first came to Chelsea I just remember coming off the tube and the grandness of it all and the smells.

I am sure everybody would be the same, when you walk up Fulham Road and the horses and the manure and all the fans and the burgers, that's my first memory of Chelsea.Going to the Shed and how enormous it was, being in the middle of it all and being quite scared with the surging of the crowd, and the smell of tobacco because everybody was smoking fags, that's what I remember.

It's bizarre but that's how I fell in love with football, the feeling of belonging which is the greatest feeling in the world.

- TIM LOVEJOY

Presenters: Tim Lovejoy and (above) David Baddiel

Basketball star: Kobe Bryant chats to Didier Drogba in the dressing room and (right) taking in a game with his LA Lakers team-mates

LAKERS' DREAM VISIT

When I was a kid growing up, I always wanted to go to an English game, but my mum wouldn't let me!

Now, 27 years later, I finally got to go to a Premier League match. I'm a big football fan and I played a lot when I was younger because I grew up in Italy – I even thought about a career in it.

I started in goal and ended up as a pretty good striker. But basketball was where my heart was.

– KOBE BRYANT

World of sport: (clockwise from top) Sprint sensation Asafa Powell, former cricketer Graham Thorpe, golfer Tiger Woods, rugby hero Lawrence Dallaglio, tennis legend Boris Becker and cricket star Kevin Pietersen

Legends of music: Bono steps out onto the pitch at Stamford Bridge and (right) Boy George gets ready to film a music video

Mane man: Boy George gets a cuddle from club mascot Stamford the Lion

POP STAR ADDS A BIT OF CULTURE

Culture Club's frontman visited Stamford Bridge in October 1984 as the group filmed a pop video during half-time of the Watford match.

His arrival prompted a bemused but light-hearted response from the Chelsea squad, with Boy George later saying: "I thought one or two were a bit macho, especially the pretty one (John Bumstead) who asked me about my hair."

David Speedie was one of those to pick up on his fashion taste, saying: He was wearing his stage clothes and he had a big hat on which was similar to one of Pat Nevin's. In fact, I'd say he was better dressed than Pat."

Joe McLaughlin added: "I must admit, when I first saw him on *Top Of The Pops* I thought: 'What a wally!' But he's basically a normal bloke underneath that make-up and strange gear."

Finally, Pat Nevin summed it up, saying: "I think he's always been as hard as nails and he was a big fella too. He didn't mind getting a bit of stick at all."

– BOY GEORGE

CFC

ONE VISIT TURNED ME INTO A BLUE

I have always hated football, but then one day, out of the blue, my son announced that he had become interested in Chelsea. However, because he spent so much time watching football on television, I started pausing to watch. For the first time ever, when conversation with friends turned to football, I could join in, instead of sticking my fingers in my ears and singing sea shanties.

This meant that pretty soon, people started asking if perhaps I'd like to go to a game. And that's why I was at Stamford Bridge watching Chelsea demolish a team called Manchester City. This was my first Premier League game and, ooh, it was good.

When you're there, rather than watching on television, you get an overall view, which means you can see how the game works.

You notice that Frank Lampard is like a blackbird, always looking around to see where the hawks are. You see that Carvalho runs with his arms up, like a begging puppy, and you work out that Michael Essien always seems to be able to find a piece of the pitch that the other team either hadn't noticed or were frightened of.

After the game I was taken to the Chelsea dressing room. I talked to Roman Abramovich, who was charming, and Lampard, who, having just run around for 90 minutes, still found the energy to get the entire team to sign my boy's Chelsea shirt.

So there we are, then. I am now a football fan. I know this because in one afternoon I learned I'm not a football fan at all. I'm a fan of Chelsea. Chelsea are the only team that can play. Stamford Bridge is my church. The men who play there are my Gods.

– JEREMY CLARKSON

Vaughan a Blue: Johnny Vaughan follows the Blues along with fellow presenter and DJ Trevor Nelson, while commentator John Motson has mixed work and pleasure at the Bridge

adidas
8
CHELSEA
FOOTBALL CLUB
SAMSUNG

Bourne a Blue: Chelsea fan and film director Paul Greengrass introduces Matt Damon to Stamford Bridge, while (left) the actor poses alongside supposed look-alike Michael Ballack and (right) fellow Hollywood star Nicole Kidman at the game

HOLLYWOOD LOOK-ALIKE

Matt Damon watching the Arsenal game with Bourne director Paul Greengrass, a season-ticket holder at the Bridge, and holding a copy of programme with Michael Ballack on cover. When told he looks like Damon, Ballack said: "I can see why people would say that, but it's actually the other way around – Matt looks like me!"

– MATT DAMON/MICHAEL BALLACK

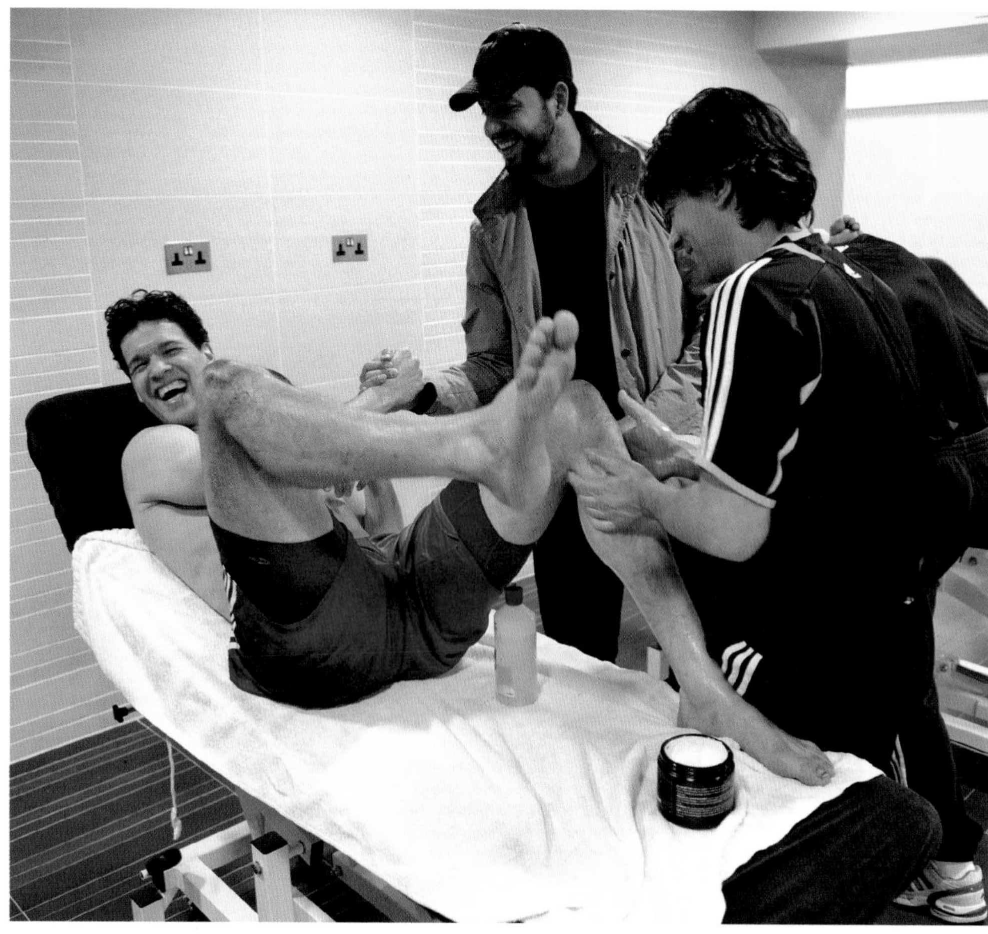

Magical experience: David Blaine shows some players a few tricks of his own during a visit to Stamford Bridge

SHOWING OFF A FEW TRICKS

Didier was really impressed with David Blaine's card tricks! He's a really good magician and you can see by Didier's reaction that he didn't see it coming. Did David tell us the secret? Of course not! But he was a cool guy, he seemed very quiet but I enjoyed talking to him.

– MICHAEL ESSIEN

L'EQUIPE
LYON VIT ENCORE
ARSENAL ET MANCHESTER BIEN PARTIS

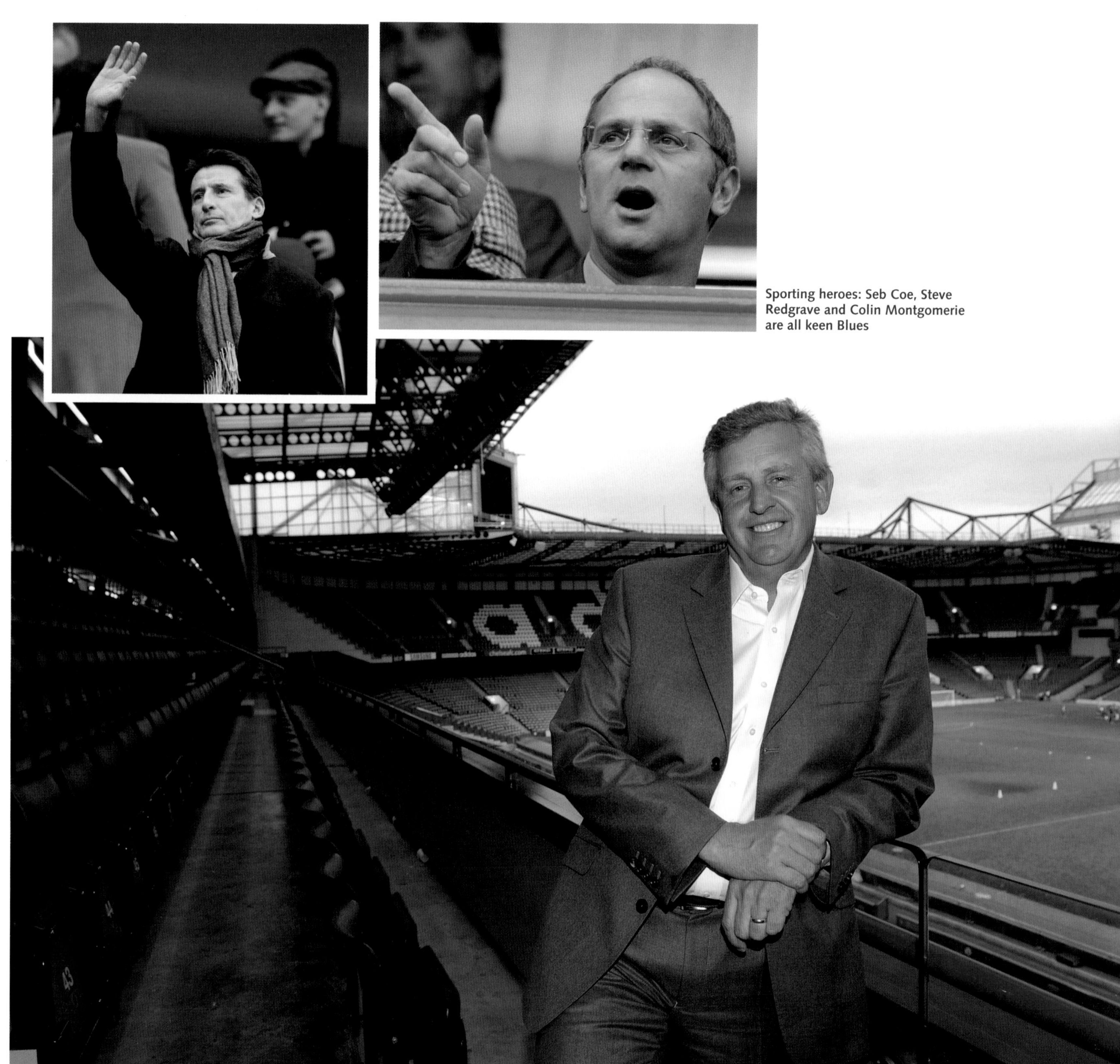

Sporting heroes: Seb Coe, Steve Redgrave and Colin Montgomerie are all keen Blues

VIP treatment: American actress Lana Turner is driven around the Bridge in May 1948 while other famous faces spotted at the ground include David Haye and football legend Pele

CHELSEA FOOTBALL CLUB
chelseafc.com

PITCHING IN

Every blade of grass gets the VIP treatment at Stamford Bridge thanks to an award-winning groundstaff, but the playing surface hasn't always been to such a high standard. The work that goes into maintaining today's manicured lawn however, is both extensive and a credit to the club...

Paint box: Groundstaff paint the lines on the pitch and (below) the team ensure the turf is brought up to standards

Bright patch: The turf gets some intense light treatment and (below) the job of relaying the pitch gets underway in 1997

Cold spell: Chelsea manager John Neal helps staff cover up the pitch in 1985

Ground force: Former groundstaff Arthur Meadows, George Anstiss and his son John Anstiss, who still works at the club in 2011

Muddy hell: Eddie McCreadie looks concerned with the playing surface back in 1977

Bubbly character: Tommy Docherty christens the Stamford Bridge centre spot with champagne ahead of the 1965/66 season

TOTALISATOR

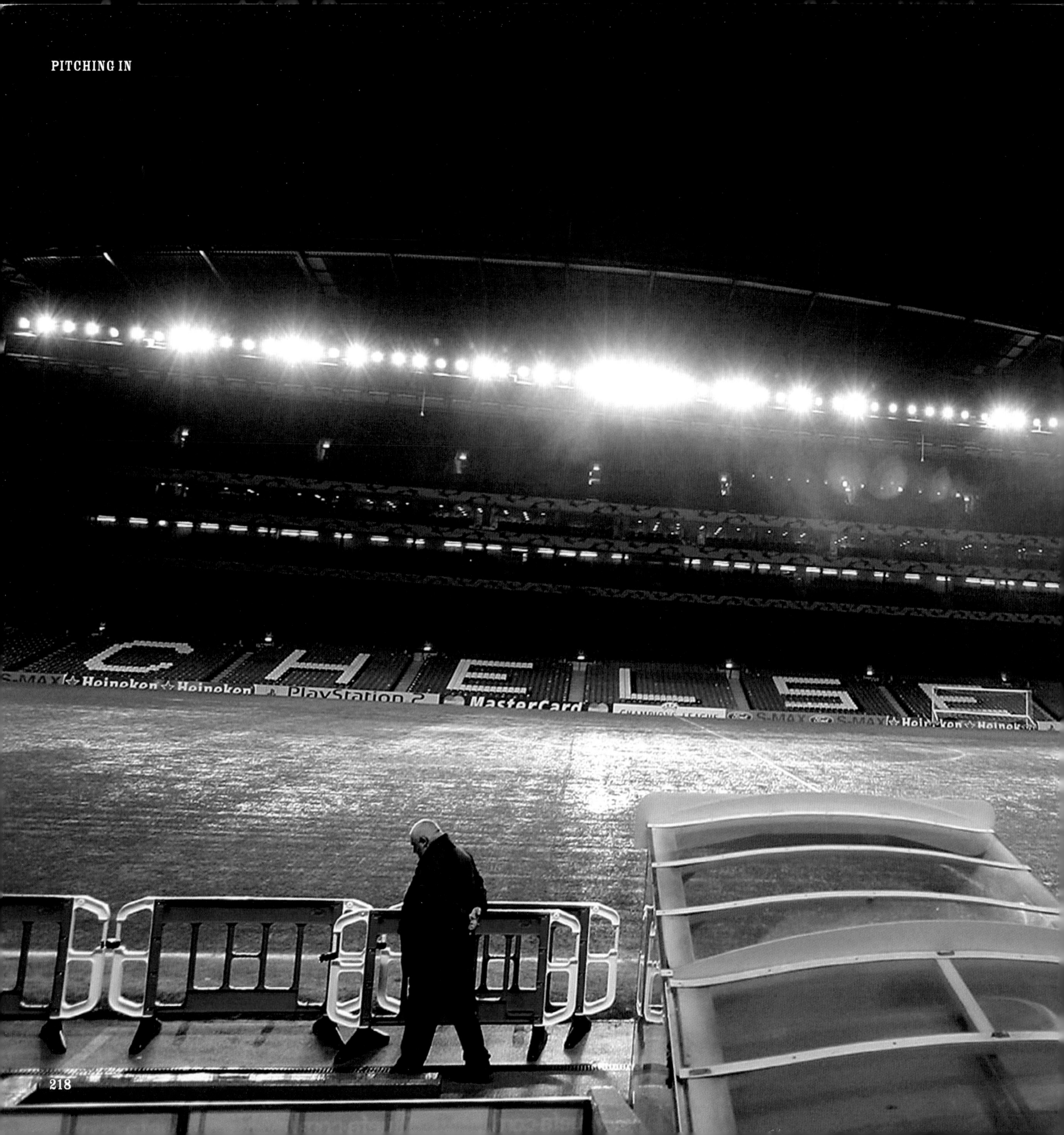
Heineken
Heineken
PlayStation 2
MasterCard

Water game: Barcelona had to contend with a heavily-watered pitch during their 1966 Fairs Cup visit, and (left) the turf gets a watering ahead a Champions League game in 2006

WATER WORKS

The real story about the second leg of the Fairs Cup against Barcelona in 1966 was us watering the pitch. We got the fire brigade down to do it. The pitch was bone hard and we thought "we're not going to win like this, let's make it difficult for them to move the ball". So the fire brigade came down and they emptied five great big fire engines all over the pitch. It was like mush when we played and Barcelona weren't too happy about it.

- JOHN HOLLINS
EX-PLAYER 1963-1975 & 1983-1984
EX-MANAGER 1985-1988

Waterlogged: The rainy weather takes its toll on the Stamford Bridge pitch in October 1988 (above) and again in February 2006 (below)

RAINY SEASON

This was a game against Fulham that was played around Christmas time in my first season. It's a nice picture – there's lots of rain.

I like playing in the rain, but when it's like this, it's too much. It can be difficult to see, it's difficult to punch the ball and to catch it. But it's English football. And football in general is a winter sport, so you just have to get used to this weather.

I like it when there is mud on the floor, we can dive on it and get dirty! And before, when I said it's typical of winter… this picture could easily have been from the summer over here!

– HILARIO

Weather the storm: Stamford Bridge under water in March 1965 (below) but the snow wasn't enough to stop the action in 1947 (bottom)

Snow joke: A blanket of snow covers the pitch in 1983, but Johnny Boyle, Terry Venables, Ron Harris and Eddie McCreadie brave the elements in training (left) in March 1965

SNOW MUST GO ON

The weather never stopped us. I don't think that years ago if there was snow you could damage the pitch anyway, because it was frozen solid. Years ago, we used to play in the snow quite a lot, but you don't see that much any more.

- RON HARRIS
EX-PLAYER 1961-1980